Business Cases for Info Pros

HERE'S WHY, HERE'S HOW

Ulla de Stricker

 Information Today, Inc.
Medford, New Jersey

First printing, 2008

Business Cases for Info Pros: Here's Why, Here's How

Library of Congress Cataloging-in-Publication Data

De Stricker, Ulla.
   Business cases for info pros : here's why, here's how / Ulla de Stricker.
      p. cm.
   Includes index.
   ISBN 978-1-57387-335-2
     1. Information services industry. 2. Information resources management.
3. Information consultants. I. Title.
   HD9999.I492D39 2008
   658.4'038--dc22

                         2008019510

President and CEO: Thomas H. Hogan, Sr.
Editor-in-Chief and Publisher: John B. Bryans
Managing Editor: Amy M. Reeve
VP Graphics and Production: M. Heide Dengler
Book Designer: Kara Mia Jalkowski
Cover Designer: Lisa Boccadutre
Copyeditor: Dorothy Pike
Proofreader: Kathleen Spaltro
Indexer: Sharon Hughes

Dedication

Every colleague and client with whom I have discussed strategic investments in information products and services over the years has been a source of inspiration for this book. In the spirit of passing on the collective wisdom so acquired, I hope readers will benefit in specific ways from its expression here.

One cherished colleague made this book a reality: Bonnie Burwell's ideas and substantial inputs—and her cheerful support when I needed an opinion—made all the difference.

Therefore, Bonnie, this book is dedicated to you.

02-22-10

The item below is now available for pickup at designated location.

Grand Rapids Public Library
zv139 GRPL Main

Baker - Allen Park
CALL NO: HD9999.I492 D39 2008
AUTHOR: De Stricker, Ulla.
Business cases for info pros : here
BARCODE: 33504005046430
REC NO: i27100888x
PICKUP AT: Main

616-406-1200

JOHN M POTTER
Grand Rapids Public Library

7:3

Contents

Introduction:
Why This Guide?

Over my more than three decades working in the information arena, I have noticed how much of a challenge it is for information professionals to establish compelling arguments for their proposals so as to achieve significant investments or budget increases. I have assisted many information professionals in planning for changes in the way they operate their information centers and offer services to clients, and one very complex part has always been the matter of getting approval for expenditures. A few key factors have stood out:

- Information professionals typically offer qualitative support that is awkward to measure in financial terms, making it difficult to arrive at tangible and credible data for use in cost/benefit analyses and return-on-investment calculations.

- The construction of an effective business case can be time-consuming; meeting the day-to-day needs of clients may leave little time for intensive study and document preparation.

- There is no proven method to follow in communicating with management. As a result, information professionals rely on their own creativity in preparing a business case for proposed investments.

Such observations led me to believe that the approach I developed in the course of my own work as a consultant might help other information professionals save time and effort. This guide uses examples from the library and information resource center domains, but these are equally applicable for professionals who function in other knowledge-intensive settings.

Anyone who needs to advance a proposal requiring support for increased budgets, reallocation of budgets, or significant capital or content investment needs a convincing case and an attention-getting presentation. The principles I illustrate are universal in that they all aim to assure decision makers of the return—financial or otherwise—that they will realize on their approval and investment.

Examples of Scenarios Calling for a Business Case

Some investments—for example, replacing aging or failing technical infrastructure—justify themselves; the negative consequences of not investing are obvious. Whenever something new is contemplated outside the "must do—or else" category, business case documents are called for. These generic examples reflect common organizational scenarios familiar to information professionals:

- Due to a significant number of employees taking early retirement, there is a shortage of corporate memory. Business teams have found themselves repeating earlier work because lessons learned from previous efforts were not identified in a timely manner. *We need a strategy and a tool or system for capturing key information objects produced in the course of the organization's work.*

- Due to the fact that the organization's business teams are spread over multiple locations or different floors, the teams sometimes arrive independently at similar project ideas and miss out on potential synergy. *We need a reliable mechanism for ensuring that each team knows what the others are planning—without adding to the information overload everyone is already experiencing.*

- Over time, as reliance on email and rapid electronic exchange of document drafts has grown, proliferation has become a major problem. Thousands of files crowd shared drives, and there are loud complaints that "we can't find the documents we need—and if we do find a document, we can't be sure it is the final official version." Everyone's time is wasted as individuals send out blanket "does anyone have a copy of ..." requests. *We need a policy and a convenient repository where official copies of non-trivial documents are safeguarded and searchable.*

- The intranet was simple and easy to navigate when it was first rolled out years ago. But now, it is widely regarded as a frustrating experience because its original structure has been compromised through ad hoc development. *We need a complete redesign—with a view to sustainability of structure.*

- The customer service agents are without a "bible" of official information they can give to customers with confidence. As a result, each customer interaction takes much longer than it ought to take, and the agents are saying they don't feel certain they are giving out the best information. *We need a central database of "correct answers" for the agents to consult as they deal with callers—along with a mechanism for updating it when new information becomes available or when agents discover new, useful insights.*

- As the organization's business emphasis has shifted and as new end-user-oriented tools are readily available on the Internet, a new assessment is needed as to what information should be purchased and licensed. *We need an audit of the current practices and of knowledge workers' actual needs so that we may plan and fund an appropriate information support strategy.*

Such frequently encountered information-related scenarios, and many more like them, call for information professionals to develop solutions or strategies and to sell them through business case documents.

How This Guide Could Help

Business Cases for Info Pros offers three types of content to assist readers in crafting a business case document according to the organizational culture in which they work:

- Information **about** business cases: the basics you need to know, a framework for identifying and planning what will go into your case, and suggestions for making it stand up to scrutiny and objection.

- An outline for gathering **key points**, with prompts on what to include and a checklist as a final verification.

- **Illustrations** intended as models for readers to adapt to their own situations.

It may be useful for the reader to skim through the entire guide quickly before paying detailed attention to those portions likely to be most relevant.

CHAPTER 1

The Decision Making Context

What Is a Business Case?

Strictly speaking, a business case is a concept; the term is analogous to "justification" or "motivation" or "potential benefits." We could say that any decision to invest in new purchases or projects is accompanied conceptually by the justification, motivation, and perception of potential benefits supporting the decision. As an example, I might think: "I will invest in a membership to this professional association [the decision]. My business case [my justification/motivation] for making the expenditure is that it will provide me with valuable benefits such as networking with colleagues, being able to attend the association's conferences and seminars, and the like." My business case in this situation is just a thought—it is not articulated as a document.

More commonly, the term "business case" refers to a *document* explaining the justification/motivation for, and anticipated benefits of, a proposed venture. As information professionals, we may have quite a few ideas up our sleeves for new positions to create in our information centers, new content to license, a revamp of the intranet, etc., but it is unlikely that such ideas will be implemented just like that. Typically, we need to create a tangible business case document explaining why our particular idea is such a good one and what benefits are expected to flow from the proposed investment in the implementation. Such a tangible document is the *instrument* through which we may achieve approval for a proposed venture—in other words, assist someone else in making a decision we favor. Before we are able to craft business case documents, however, we need to understand the context for the making of a decision.

What Is the Context for the Decision?

This chapter discusses the *context* in which decisions get made. As we build our factual business cases, we must not lose sight of the fact that decision makers in some cases are motivated by subtle considerations not necessarily tightly connected to the bare facts presented in our proposal document.

First, I illustrate a decision to be made entirely within our own mental purview. In other words, I am familiar with the situation at hand, and I need no one else's approval to proceed with my choice.

Second, I show how it's more difficult to decide when the facts and ramifications are not familiar to the decider—the very situation our readers are in when they receive our business case document!

Finally, I lead into the body of the guide by commenting on some key considerations to keep in mind regarding decision makers' requirements when it comes to reacting to proposals from us.

To Begin: Why Do We Prepare a Business Case?

In short, we prepare a business case because passion alone is not sufficient. A business case articulation is our instrument for bringing about a desired business decision in that it provides a means for decision makers to evaluate potential investments on the basis of data and reason. It provides our management a foundation for informed decisions about what to fund, what to cut, and how to set priorities by doing the following:

- Defining an opportunity to be exploited or a problem to be solved

- Proposing an approach or a solution and outlining objectives and scope

- Describing alternatives to be considered

- Providing estimates for needed resources, scheduling, and costs

- Quantifying tangible gains (to the degree possible) and describing intangible benefits

- Considering any risks and identifying options for their mitigation

- Positioning the proposed approach in light of the competitive outlook

When It's Our Own Decision

Within the authority domain of our individual work lives, we make dozens of decisions every day without even necessarily thinking of them as decisions: what time to suggest for a meeting and who should be invited, whether to print on both sides of the paper, whether to keep looking for more information or stop now, which of three office supply companies to go with, how to rate a staff member in an evaluation, which of several conferences to have a key staff member attend, etc. Wherever alternatives exist, we arrive at a choice as a result of weighing the advantages, future ramifications, and costs (not necessarily financial) of each. Whether they are routine and rapid ("since this has been a good choice in the past, I'll stick with what I know works") or require some reflection and calculation, in the end the decision is one we feel serves the need or aspiration at hand with the fewest downsides (e.g., I prefer to avoid early morning meetings; we're a green office, so double-sided printing sends the right message, etc.).

In such straightforward decisions, we are fully aware of every aspect of the "business case." We know the reasons a given choice offers benefits, and we know the downsides of other potential choices.

Should decisions be more complex, we likely seek input to help increase our confidence that we are making the right choice. A major motivator here is the distaste we have for regret. We would rather not face the thought of "I should have chosen the other option" at a later time, much less the thought of having to justify a choice in front of stakeholders who consider it ill-advised.

In the case of matters with ramifications beyond the immediate low-risk environment, we may engage in extended rounds of consultation to ensure that we (1) have buy-in from a broad representation of stakeholders, and (2) can support our decision with budgetary calculations and projections.

Regardless how trivial or significant the matter we need to decide on, in the absence of major extrinsic factors exerting influence (it's only three months until the office move, so it makes sense to get the new equipment at that time), we typically select the path we believe will move us forward toward overall goals—or away from upcoming difficulties—with the least effort and risk and at the lowest cost.

Therefore, we could say we are expert decision makers within our own business areas. But let's pause here to look at some of the questions that enter into a typical decision, even though we may be conscious of them for only a few moments.

Example of a Decision When the Implications Are Familiar

The upcoming retirement of two staff members has created the need for planning and consultations with staff in the department's two offices (East Coast and West Coast). **I need to decide:** How should I stage the necessary consultations so that everyone feels heard—at the lowest cost?

Having received commentary from various individuals advancing their preferences regarding meeting logistics, I have an idea of the stakeholders' existing considerations. Narrowing the options down (and assuming that a traditional telephone conference call just isn't going to cut it for this matter), I now weigh the pros and cons of each:

1. Logistics/cost

    a. Hold one meeting—fly the West Coast people in

    b. Hold two meetings—fly myself to the West Coast

2. Attendance/implications

    a. Invite managers and knowledge workers

    b. Invite all staff

Option	Considerations	
	PRO	**CON**
1a	Great benefit for the two offices to work closely together—helps ongoing effort to align them.	Costly—can only afford to fly out *X* number of people, which leaves out some staff whose input is valuable.
	Any consideration can be discussed in the light of ramifications for both offices—that might not be known to either group in isolation.	The expenditure, in light of other areas where restraint is mandated, may appear frivolous.

	Gesture toward West Coast office's occasional comments that it feels "second."	
1b	Shows cost consciousness to purchase only one airfare; I could stay a few more days to stress the importance I give to this matter. I will have the opportunity to spend time with each person individually.	If the boss is the only one to visit the West Coast office, is it credible that all views from there have received adequate consideration (how well can I summarize the input)? Given that I have visited on several occasions before, there could be a risk that this visit is seen as no more important than previous ones.
2a	The potential changes could cause some anxiety among some staff, so perhaps it's best to phase the discussions for now. There is a need to discuss freely any ramifications for operational staff.	If involvement is limited, there is vulnerability to a charge of exclusions. Any time operational staff members perceive they are left out, they tend to worry unduly.
2b	An all-staff session supports the message of inclusiveness that has been fostered all along. Often, in such an open forum, many good ideas emerge spontaneously.	An open forum requires greater effort to manage expectations—not every idea voiced will be carried out, and there could be disappointment. An open forum may set off a wave of speculation taking on a life of its own (different from the speculation that may ensue from 1a).

Now, what combination will I choose? 1a2a, 1a2b, 1b2a, 1b2b?

Difficult as our independent decisions may be, they are still confined to our own judgment and weighing of each option's pros and cons. We don't have to prepare essays setting out the nuances of the risks and rewards that could ensue from each option combination because we "instantly" understand them, being intimately familiar with the overall territory and the recent history of the environment.

Example of a Decision When the Implications Are Unfamiliar

But what if we must make a decision based on someone else's information? In such a case, we do not have the benefit of personal impressions formed over time, nor a strong sense of the potential ramifications of each option.

In the context of deciding on meeting logistics, my staff propose a different approach using a Web-based collaboration tool. While I am aware of Web-based collaboration tools in a general sense, it had not occurred to me to consider them outside the context of technical teamwork. **I need to decide:** Is a technology-based solution right for us in this situation?

My staff point out three benefits:

1. Logistics/cost: Save considerable money by avoiding air travel—build a collaborative culture for the future.

   a. Obtain Web-based collaborative tool, and orient everyone in its use.

   b. Then hold Web-based meetings—everyone can "write on the whiteboard" and hear each other.

2. Attendance/implications: Everyone participates—real time and by prior/subsequent email.

   a. Prepare a set of fundamental questions, and invite everyone to comment on them in the Web collaboration space prior to the Web meetings.

   b. After the Web meetings, hold post-mortem Web updates.

3. Future gains: Web meeting tools will serve us well in many projects in the future.

a. The two offices will be able to work much more closely together.

b. Over time, the ongoing reduction in travel costs will be significant.

Item	Benefits (Investment)
1a	The investment for X number of seats to the software amounts to only $\$Y$, which in comparison to airfare is quite attractive. Our return on that investment is a factor of how well we leverage the tool in day-to-day operations.
1b	Once everyone has scaled the learning curve, it's "open season," and we can use the tool for any and all occasions when we need to communicate and collaborate. A downstream benefit will be that at any time, we can garner the input and engagement from many more participants in the two offices than we have been able to obtain earlier.
2a	Specifically for this round of meetings, we have the opportunity to do "pre" and "post" events to augment the depth of participation and discussion. Asking everyone to comment on basic questions in advance will help enhance the quality of commentary because the comments are seen in a shared forum—not just submitted to one person. The actual Web meeting, where everyone can hear what is being said while they look at documents, can thus be much more productive because of the prior sharing (precious on-air decision time is not wasted with clarifications that could have been handled earlier).
2b	Once the Web meeting has taken place and management decisions have been made, information can flow to all teams so that it is clear how everyone's input affected the final decision. Experience shows that team members value *being heard* more than they value *getting their way*.

3a	Over time, the Web collaboration tool enables us to minimize the sense of separation between the two offices, because in essence, any two or more people can congregate and discuss things any time they like. It's not quite a water cooler, but it's close.
3b	As we all get used to the virtual collaboration, it is reasonable to assume that travel between the offices can decline by $X-Y\%$, for ongoing savings in the $\$Z$ range.

Now, having been exposed to virtual collaboration tools in other settings, but not having managed this type of stakeholder input process before, will I approve the proposed approach for the planning exercise, based on the benefits explained?

The experience of making a decision based on unfamiliar input from others is good preparation for moving toward the task of advocating a decision for someone else to make.

When It's Not Our Decision

When we are required to present a case for decision making by others, we can't be certain about the insights and corporate memory that may sway the decision makers' deliberations. Thus, we are without the luxury of mental shortcuts!

Advancing a proposal for approval "upstairs" or by an external group of stakeholders is a significant challenge because we must shed light—fairly—on every component aspect in such a way that individuals not necessarily familiar with the details may nevertheless be able to reason their way to a decision they (1) are comfortable accepting themselves, and (2) could champion further up the line if need be.

In my experience, the task of creating an instrument for decision making by others is indeed a good example of the "devil is in the details." The instrument must meet a range of requirements in that it must not only:

- Set out the pertinent facts objectively and concisely—but without glossing over detail

- Paint a clear and neutral picture of the available options (including doing nothing)

- Credibly explain why some potential options were disregarded at the outset

but it must also:

- Explain benefits and risks, properly weighed against each other

- Clarify what is fact based and what is judgment based

- Stand up to scrutiny as to any extrinsic motivators

- Establish a comfort level on the part of decision makers so that they are on firm ground in making their choice

- Provide sufficient "meat" with which they could champion our case

If we are keenly invested in a particular outcome, it may be particularly difficult to advocate while still maintaining objectivity. Sometimes, we may need to swallow the business reality that what we see as an untoward decision may in fact be acceptable to decision makers, given their overall focus.

The View from "Upstairs"

In some environments, consensus decision making is favored. That does not obviate the need for a solid business case. In the following, I use the "upstairs" metaphor to designate the decision making entity, regardless whether it really is "up" in the organization or "sideways" to a team of peers.

A key point of departure for shaping any proposal is to put oneself in the manager's shoes, asking "how does my idea look from here?" We must recognize that no matter how obviously good our proposal is in our own view, there has to be something in it for those to whom we pitch it.

Imagine the following immediate reactions to our proposal on the part of managers upstairs:

- No doubt the addition of a quiet room would alleviate the congestion and noise in the main seating area, but the budget does not allow for any such capital expense.

- Adding two more professional librarians to the team would go a long way toward enhancing the overall level of knowledge for decision making, but it's difficult to tie two new salaries to any tangible outcome on the bottom line.

- The content proposed for licensing is certainly relevant, but how will we realize or measure a return on the steep license fee?

Such reactions illustrate the business reality that "nice to have" may not hold sway with shareholders or those in charge of budgets. Their sights could be trained squarely on quarterly earnings or tight budget constraints.

Therefore, our proposals need to contain that vital additional ingredient often referred to as WIIFT, or "What's in it for them?" How can we entice others to approve and go to bat for our idea?

Motivations Matter

The number one request business managers make when it comes to proposals is: "Please don't make me do the work." In other words: "Make it easy for me to see how I can safely advance the proposal on your behalf and look smart while I'm doing it. I have no appetite for poring over pages and pages, attempting to interpret the key business drivers—nor for looking unprepared in championing a shaky case."

Addressing WIIFT may require insight into the true motivations of executives, or the lack thereof. Consider the following circumstances an executive might be contemplating:

- In my last three years here, I would like to put in place a solid legacy. This knowledge management initiative has been talked about for quite some time … I will now make sure to be the one to see it to fruition.

- If the expansion of the information center can be linked to significant reductions in time-to-market … I'll stick my neck out by sponsoring it.

or:

- Punishing budget cuts have been announced across the board. Now is not the time to even think about increased spending.

- With the costly replacement of our entire IT infrastructure, next year will be a better time for the initiative in the information center.

What Management Needs Before Acting on a Recommendation: Making the Sale

Given the perspective from upstairs, it is reasonable that management needs to be *sold* on our ideas. To echo the well-known anecdote about selling what's in the skin cream jar—moisturizer—versus selling something entirely different—the dream of better looking skin—we need to understand whether there are *selling points* we should feature. No doubt you have heard variations on how "the house was well priced, well located, recently renovated, and so on … but what sold it were the hydraulic drawers in the kitchen."

I make this point not to suggest that business cases contain "advertising" but to stress the reality that they are sales instruments. In life and at work, people do what they perceive will lead to something desirable for themselves or for their constituencies in the context of their business deliverables. It is our job to point to the benefits and gains we can deliver, and it is an advantage if in addition we can appeal to overall organizational aspirations.

Examples of some common areas toward which we could pitch a proposal's selling features include an organization leader's:

- Role as a visionary leader and morale builder

- Desire for a track record as a responsible manager who is able to control costs

- Concern about regulatory requirements

- Need to attract and keep a younger workforce in a competitive industry

- Goal of developing a compelling new product or service

- Long-term strategy of moving into a new market

Knowing what personal or corporate selling features will resonate is a matter of being highly attuned to the prevailing perceptions in the environment and the overall corporate culture in an organization.

Influence Politics: Grassroots Support

Just as we know not to open new subjects as surprises in meetings—we first get everyone on board one by one—so, too, should proposals from out of nowhere be avoided. Talking up the background and reasons why "we need to do something about *X*" well in advance of submitting a proposal can go a long way toward getting an *invitation* to submit a proposal and then toward smoothing the way to its approval. There is considerable comfort for decision makers in recognizing "oh yes, I've been hearing about this for a while now, and the idea seems to have a number of aspects in its favor." In addition, discussing an idea at the grassroots level enables us to find out about the potential objections and risks so we can demonstrate that we know about them and have allowed for them in the proposal.

Pre-selling requires considerable social capital and the backup of others. It is helpful if there is a general impression that "oh, if Iris Ganning is positive toward the idea, it really must be worth considering." How is social capital accumulated? Carefully, over time, as we demonstrate our value and trustworthiness to individuals and teams in the course of supporting the business of the enterprise. Those who have mastered the art of relationship management, building bridges across a community of individuals, can testify to the considerable informal influence they have earned as a result.

Influence Politics: The Senior Champion or Thought Leader

An even more powerful element of social support is the senior-level champion or respected opinion leader who will espouse our case. Attaining an *a priori* supporter may be beyond most of us, but if the opportunity should appear, be sure to make the most of it … and above all, be sure not to let the supporter down with a less-than-stellar document!

Champions may appear or be cultivated as the result of chance encounters or other circumstantial factors (there may be a shared sports interest, his or her spouse may be involved in a community event we are working on, or we may both be on the United Way campaign team). That is one good reason to have an "elevator speech" or sound bite ready at all times.

As a note of caution: We should not rely exclusively on a senior champion. For all we know, our champion could be off on another assignment or for any other reason suddenly be absent.

What's Next?

Using the familiar scenario of deciding how to spend our personal money, we consider rationales and justifications commonly associated with the deliberations attached to significant expenditures. Any case for investing money needs a solid set of motivations and benefits to make the decision come about.

CHAPTER 2

Thinking About Money

In our day-to-day lives, we constantly prioritize our personal purchases and investments. The process often entails a justification of expenditures, particularly when the amount in question is significant.

Crafting a business case similarly involves rationales and motivations, so that decision makers may arrive at a comfort level where they feel confident making an investment.

Personal Scenario: Buying a Family Car

Using various facets of a scenario involving the purchase of a new car, the following list gives examples of ways in which we justify our personal purchase decisions. In the next section, these examples are "translated" into the environment of a business case.

Here are some thoughts by a couple, whose first child is expected in five months, perusing the dealer catalogues and wandering through showrooms:

1. **This expenditure is *cost effective.*** We will save on gas and car repairs—the old clunker is such a gas guzzler. Over X number of years, the net cost of the new car will only be Y—less than it is costing now to run the old car.

2. **The expense is a good *investment.*** This new car has good resale value, so there is some upside at the end of the first four years or so when it may be time to trade it in.

3. **There are some *indirect (non-monetary) benefits* to making the purchase.** The safety of our children is paramount, and this car has an excellent safety record.

4. **The expenditure will allow** *downstream benefits.* Many of the neighbors don't own cars. If we show good neighborliness and offer to take along others on the drive into town, we are in a better position to ask to borrow a snow blower.

5. **Now is the** *right time* **to make the purchase.** The dealers are clearing the current year's models; now is the best time to buy.

6. **The purchase** *fits with other decisions* **we have recently made.** Buying a new, reliable car fits in well with starting a family. We want to trust our transportation when we have other matters demanding our attention.

7. **We** *already have a portion of the investment* **available.** The small inheritance from Uncle Frank will help with the purchase. As an alternative, the banker expressed a willingness to help extend the line of credit.

8. **We should** *compare and evaluate* **this purchase in terms of other expenditures we have been making.** The house we bought last year requires a longer commute, so a safe and cost effective car is appropriate.

Business Scenario: Investing in a License for Information Content

Making a business case frequently entails asking for additional resources; in doing so, we rationalize and justify expenditures to management. We can apply how we thought about purchase justification in a personal scenario.

Following is a "translation" of the car purchasing scenario into a scenario involving a request for funding to acquire new content in a corporate information center (a scenario we will revisit in Case Study 3 in Chapter 6):

1. **This expenditure is** *cost effective.* Certain existing expenditures will become unnecessary with this new content in place.

2. **The expense is a good** *investment.* It is estimated that the investment will reduce by several hours per week the amount of time knowledge workers are each spending in hunting for information. That translates to a productivity gain of X per year overall.

3. **There are some *indirect benefits* to making this purchase.** Moving in this direction puts us in line with what our competitors are doing; we need to do this if we are truly interested in "hiring the best in the field." The license will allow us to be totally ethical in our information use; we know we will be in compliance with legal and regulatory requirements. It is difficult to put a price tag on the reduction of staff stress and frustration, but this is the kind of initiative that could improve staff "wellness" and thus have a beneficial effect on productivity.

4. **This expenditure will allow *downstream benefits*.** There is the potential that the acquisition of new content resources will permit us to market and sell our research services to additional clients.

5. **Now is the *right time* to make this purchase.** The vendor is willing to negotiate substantially on the cost of the trial service if we are able to go ahead with the initiative this year; significant savings are possible.

6. **This purchase *fits with other decisions* we have recently made.** The license will leverage our investment in new portal technology.

7. **We can get *assistance* to make this purchase.** A director has indicated his willingness to contribute $X from his department's budget toward the prototype. Funds for the portal implementation could logically be directed to the new content as well.

8. **We should *compare and evaluate* this purchase in terms of other expenditures we have been making.** When we compare the expenditure to those for other corporate services, we note, as an example, that monthly cell phone costs per employee are in excess of our cost estimates for the new content.

Positioning a Request for Money: Up Front or at the End?

Naturally, we cannot simply state a request such as "Please authorize an expenditure of $Y." The recipient is entitled to information about the reasons and the anticipated returns. The question then arises: Do we elaborate the reasons and payoffs *prior to* issuing the request for a given investment amount, in effect leading the decision maker gently through the rationale and the benefit in an effort to guard against sticker shock? Or do we issue the request up front, in effect letting the decision maker in on the scope right away?

The corporate culture may provide guidance. It could be advisable to be fairly upfront; in today's busy environment, decision makers do not want to spend significant time reading through a document before finding out how much they are asked to approve. One decision maker expressed a preference memorably: "Don't waste my time by keeping the amount a secret until the last page. Tell me how much you want; then tell me what I'm going to get for my money—in two, maximum three pages."

Is It Advisable to Provide Multiple Investment Options?

In some cultures, it is expected that a business case will set out options so that decision makers have a way of assessing the ramifications of a decision to approve a partial but not the full recommended investment. Typically referred to as the bronze-silver-gold approach, this technique has advantages and disadvantages:

- **Pro:** Offering a description of "What can be had for what investment" provides context at the outset, obviating the need for follow-up communication triggered by "But are there no alternatives? What if the budget won't accommodate the request?" Moreover, it shows that thought has been given to scenarios other than the ideal one.

- **Con:** Showing multiple options could lead to an instinctive selection of the least expensive one. Unless the bronze option is the one we realistically expect to obtain and the silver and gold ones are added in to make the bronze option look attractive, we could inadvertently provide a reason for decision makers not to commit to what we are requesting.

On balance, the best advice may be to follow a simple path: Advocate for what you know is the right thing to do; then, recognizing that resources may not suffice, offer a less expensive alternative you could still support—in the short term, that is. We do not want to signal that less-than-ideal solutions are acceptable. Thus, the message focuses on scalability: "Here is what is needed. If the budget cannot accommodate it right now, an acceptable alternative—*as we gear up over a longer time frame*—would be to phase in the investments."

A key consideration is to avoid creating the perception that we are asking decision makers to do our work. A business case is the result of careful analysis, not an invitation to others to perform tasks that are within our responsibility.

What's Next?

Now let us turn to the practical aspects of preparing a business case document. In the next chapter, we look at "what a business case document *is*" and at some overall suggestions for writing one.

CHAPTER 3

The Business Case Approach

What Is Included in a Business Case?

As noted in Chapter 1, a business case document is an instrument for securing approval for a proposed action and the associated investment (not always financial). Therefore, the business case document typically contains certain elements:

- A business case is a proposal to suggest and justify changes, initiatives, or investments. It may also be aimed at solving problems; that is, it may identify and analyze the cause of an organizational problem and recommend a solution.

- A business case document is a call to pursue a proposed direction and a statement of a related benefit for an audience: "*X* is a good idea for the department and for the organization because ..."

- Sometimes, a business case advocates *against* a proposed untoward change by defending (at least some part of) the status quo and outlining why the change is *not* a good idea: "If the budget were indeed cut, the following services will be impacted in such a way as to limit access to ..., which in turn would mean that employees can no longer ..."

On the other hand, be aware of pitfalls:

- A business case does not simply describe a situation that is undesirable from the point of view of its writer.

- It is not a general expression of "wouldn't it be nice if ..."

- It is not a defense against real or imagined suggestions that performance in a department is not up to par. (Should there be such concerns, a business case will positively describe the actions necessary for achieving a favorable outcome.)

- It is not a request for readers to do the work of choosing among several alternatives. (We show why *our preferred option* is the way to go.)

What Is the Overall Process of Writing a Business Case?

The overall process of writing a business case is as follows:

1. Prepare politically. As noted previously, a business case should never come "out of the blue." Do not go to the work of preparing one until you have discussed it with your most immediate stakeholders (your manager, colleagues, best customers), so that you know there is a chance your initiative will be well received, in whole or in part.

2. Study. Scan the *Business Case Framework* in Chapter 4. Read the case studies in Chapter 6, following along with the framework to see how the cases reflect the outline and suggestions. Then, plot in general how your case would be similar or different.

3. Review the framework in more detail, this time highlighting and noting the components you want to include in your own document.

4. Determine the format and size of your written case according to organizational culture.

5. Think about where you will find the information you need for your case. Identify the individuals you will involve in preparing it.

6. If it is possible, share your draft version and seek input from colleagues, a mentor, or a champion before you submit the document to decision makers.

7. Review your completed document, using the final checklist in the Afterword as a guide.

Whose Help Should I Seek in Preparing Work on the Business Case?

As you gather information for your business case, seek out assistance. Documented involvement of and commentary from relevant stakeholders and other authoritative individuals will add to the credibility of your case. Involve relevant others, for example:

- Finance staff for assistance with budget and cost analyses

- IT staff for any proposals that require the acquisition of new technology or will have impact on existing technology (and thus also future technology plans)

- Human Resources staff for advice on personnel matters such as compensation

- Vendors (if you are proposing licensing new content or acquiring new tools)

- Members of your professional community who have undertaken similar initiatives

- Knowledge workers whose productivity could improve with new investments (e.g., in systems or desktop tools)

A Business Case Example Close to Home

For a straightforward business case analogy, let's listen to two high school students present a case to their respective parents as to why they need approval and funds to go backpacking "starting in Thailand where Barbara's cousin lives" for eight months before they enter university. The soon-to-be-grads have an innate sense how a business proposal goes as they speak to their parents:

- **Background**: As parents, you always stressed how important it is for us to see the world and gain insight into other cultures and societies. We're not sure what to choose for a major, and we need some time to find ourselves ... besides, we're burned out, so going to college right away might just waste the tuition ... we could end up dropping out and living at home.

- **Proposal**: We want to defer our freshman year at ABC University and join Barbara and Rafi on their second trek to the Far East. They figure it will cost about $X all told, for airfare to Thailand and back, local transportation, food, and hostel accommodations for the eight months. If we work as scuba diving instructors along the way, like Catherine did last year, we can reduce that amount considerably or make it go a lot further.

- **Risks of Business as Usual**: If we don't go, we'll miss out on a huge opportunity to expand our horizons. We may never have this opportunity to travel with experienced backpackers again. Besides, it's generally not advised these days to go straight from high school into college.

- **Downsides of Some Obvious Alternatives**: We considered the Europe trip, but we feel we won't learn much, and the cost would be five times higher!

- **Benefits of the Proposal**: We'll have a chance to get some perspective and gain some maturity so that when we do start freshman year, we'll really be able to get into studying.

- **Ancillary Benefits**: In this global economy, it's important to have contacts all over the world. Also, international travel is a plus when it comes to getting into graduate school and getting jobs.

- **Reasonable Investment**: We have some money saved from our summer jobs, and we're selling our cars—so all we're asking for is $Y. That's cheaper than feeding us at home!

- **Risk Mitigation**: We already thought of it. We'll carry GPS phones, and since we'll be four traveling together, it's unlikely we'll be at risk. We promise to call home twice a week and to stick to well-traveled routes.

(The part about how many times they'll mow the lawn won't apply here, as we can't "sweeten the deal" for our managers the way teens like to do for their parents!)

Suggestions to Guide You as You Write

A business case has a lot in common with a mountain climbing guide: It must take readers from ground level up through the various way stations to the top, where the "grand vision" is—and keep them comfortable, secure, and oriented every step of the way. In that context, here is a series of general guidelines with their rationale.

Make Sure the Focus Is on Your Organization— Not Your Department

You are selling—an idea, a solution, an opportunity, a defense. *Selling* means that you focus on the needs and wants of the person or group you are addressing. Try to understand the perspectives of your stakeholders: If you were in their shoes, what would your concerns and objections be? Take yourself and your department out of the focus and shift it to the recipient. Start with, and stick with, the idea of "*the organization gets*" rather than "*I would like.*"

Put Your Fundamental Mission Up Front—Concisely

Lack of time is a major problem in most organizations. Few readers will have time to carefully review the whole of your proposal. Unless it is in the form of a brief memo, every proposal should have an executive summary that can stand alone.

Emphasize the Benefits—Clearly

In order to raise interest and engagement, present clear benefits before getting into operational detail. You want the readers to think, "I like this prospect" before you cover the duller details of how your department's day-to-day activities would change.

Don't Ignore or Play Down Potential Constraints or Problems

Most ideas have some potentially challenging or at least "interesting" aspects. By acknowledging them and showing how they can be dealt with, you may gain support. If any constraints are associated with costs, you need to show how the proposal's benefits will outweigh those costs. The guideline here is to follow the "already considered that" approach to demonstrate you have thought things through. Readers appreciate seeing their concerns validated, and heading off potential objections right away in the proposal may shorten any negotiation period considerably.

Know the Organization's Expectations for the Format and Length of a Business Case

Every organization exhibits its own practice for evaluating potential investments. Your chances of approval are greater if you conform to expectations and requirements for business case documents. There can be a temptation to throw "everything but the kitchen sink" into a business case, but if a memo is acceptable, make it a memo. If the expectation is for a full-blown proposal complete with budgets, then a memo will not cut it.

Use Clear, Active, Powerful Language

To get your message across, you need to use clear, concrete, and compelling language that will be readily understood by readers:

- Employ active, bold language. You want your proposal to pack punch.

- Avoid clichés, outmoded fad expressions, and "business speak."

- If specialized terms are needed, explain them in lay language. (In particular, library jargon is unhelpful. For example, the term "acquisitions" means something else outside this milieu—consider using "procurement of electronic content and such print materials as are not available in electronic form").

Use Stories and Quotes from Others in Similar Situations

A concrete story tends to grab attention. Quotes bring it home that your proposal is not a construct but has "legs" in others' experience. Readers may appreciate knowing that they are not in experimental territory, and it reflects well on you to have examined what others have done.

Be Specific and Use Quantifications Whenever Possible

Quantifications, although they may well be estimates, tend to have more impact than general statements. Compare the following statements from the point of view of persuasiveness:

> Employees will save a significant amount of time in seeking information.

vs.

> The two hours per week knowledge workers are estimated to save in seeking information will result in a productivity gain translating to a potential 5,000 hours per year that could be devoted to priority deliverables.

Provide the Opportunity for Approval of Portions
or Phases of a Proposal

In the case of larger projects, it could be advantageous to structure the proposal, so that it is not an all-or-nothing proposition but leaves the door open for management to select a gradual approach.

For example, in a strategic planning study to determine long-term business and service strategy, phases could be considered:

- Phase 1 is a feasibility assessment to clarify certain parameters for the purposes of verifying assumptions about scopes and costs.

- Phase 2 is a first-round study involving priority stakeholders to create a baseline of knowledge about their concerns and preferences.

- Phase 3 extends the study to the remaining participant groups.

As another example, in a proposal for purchasing or licensing content, the proposal could incorporate a proof-of-concept, pilot, or trial stage to ensure that assumptions are valid, to learn lessons for a broader deployment, and to adjust budgets if necessary. That is the approach taken in Case Study 3 in Chapter 6.

What's Next?

The next chapter outlines the segments to include in a business case and their sequence, as well as the type of content to be included in each segment of the case.

CHAPTER 4

The Business Case Framework

The following outline is a framework to be adapted to *your* needs and situation:

- You may choose not to include all of the segments outlined.

- You may want to change the order in which the segments are presented.

- As you review the suggestions on the type of content to include in each of the segments, you may vary from the amount of detail proposed.

- Questions are posed to prompt you to think about your own situation; not all will be relevant to your business case or require answers that must be included in your case.

- You may want to present certain types of information in appendices rather than in the body of the business case.

Considerations Regarding the Style of the Business Case

To help you determine what, and how much, information should go into your business case, consider the following:

- The type of organization you work in: corporate, government, or nonprofit. Government workplaces typically require a significant amount of supporting data while corporate workplaces may demand brevity. Nonprofit organizations often fall between the two, depending on size and governance structure.

- The size and complexity of your organization or of your part of it.

- The culture: low-key and informal, or more structured and formal?

- The standard communication format for all types of exchanges in your organization: Everything in formal writing? A brief memo? A discussion, with supporting materials, at a monthly meeting with a manager?

- Organizational expectations: Is preparation of a business case document a common practice in your organization? If so, what form does it typically take? (A written memo prepared prior to a meeting? A presentation to a management board? A full-blown, bound report?)

- Existence of style guides: Does your organization already have templates or guides for preparation of proposals that you are required to use? If so, you will be able to employ the suggestions for content in this guide to complete your required template.

Table of Contents

Your business case document will contain at least some of the segments suggested here as a potential table of contents:

1. Executive Summary

2. Background

3. Environmental Analysis

4. Options: Pros and Cons

5. Proposed Approach

6. Budget and Cost Analysis

7. Benefits

8. Strategic Alignment and Risk Mitigation

9. Readiness to Proceed

10. Appendices

In the following tables, the key elements in each document segment are outlined in the left column; the right column gives examples for clarification (that is, the right-hand column is not a comprehensive list).

1. Executive Summary

Nature of this segment: A brief overview of your business case, easily digestible by busy readers.

Although listed as the first segment of your business case—because that is where it will appear in a written proposal—the summary is written *after* the other segments have been prepared so that all essential ideas are captured in the Executive Summary.

Key Points to Include	Comments and Examples
• A concise statement of exactly what you are proposing	**Proposal**: *Two new positions are proposed for the information center in order to meet sharply increased requirements for information support to knowledge workers.*
• The drivers for the proposal: the problem to be resolved, the need to be filled, or the opportunity to be pursued (PNO)	**Drivers**: *The competitive environment and business expansion have in recent years led to growth in the number of knowledge workers. The information center can no longer support the demand for research support and current market monitoring, thus exposing knowledge workers to considerable time waste and missed opportunities. A study showed that knowledge workers spend on average 2–3 hours per week in unproductive pursuit of information because the information center is understaffed—translating into $X of wasted knowledge worker salaries.*

• The effort and investment in terms of dollars, time, and people required to implement your proposal	**Investment**: *Two new positions are estimated to cost in the range of $Y annually; a removal of little-used materials to the offsite records facility will provide the necessary space.*
• The key benefits to be realized	**Benefits**: *Appropriate information support will enhance productivity and address competitive pressures by enabling business teams to: (1) assess project viability with greater confidence, and (2) shorten project completion times.*

2. Background

Nature of this segment: Summary of the current situation and problem, need, or opportunity (PNO).

Key Points to Include	Comments and Examples
• What the problem, need, or opportunity is • Evidence the PNO exists • How the PNO originated • What's not optimal about the status quo: negative consequences of the current situation—or downsides of not taking advantage of an opportunity • If relevant, why any previous attempts at solutions did not work	Be clear about the **nature** of the drivers for your business case. *Is a **problem** serious enough that it must be addressed formally?* *Have you identified specific **needs** on the part of staff or clients whose fulfillment is material to the organization?* *Is there an **opportunity** you want to pursue for the benefit of the organization?* If a **problem** is the driver, identify root causes—the best solutions address the true cause of a problem. *How did the problem originate?* *What has been its history?* *How are the readers involved or impacted?*

	If **needs** are unmet, describe the negative consequences of the current situation and quantify as much as possible through accurate and current statistics, facts, and examples. Let's say demand for services has outstripped the number of staff in the information center:
	What services are you unable to deliver, in whole or in part?
	For what client groups are you unable to meet all needs? With what consequences?
	What unnecessary costs are being incurred?
	What is the impact on personnel? Are wasted hours or repeated work, for example, a hindrance to competitiveness?
	If **opportunity** is the driver:
	Exactly what is the opportunity?
	What circumstances have made the opportunity possible at this time?
	What beneficial prospects are attached to pursuing the opportunity at this time?

3. Environmental Analysis

Nature of this segment: An indication that the situation described in the Background section is not unique to your organization—or an indication that your organization's situation differs in certain ways from other organizations' situations.

Key Points to Include	Comments and Examples
External Facts	
• What **competitive pressures and regulatory issues** are having an impact?	Establish the point that the request for investment is driven not by a personal desire but rather by environmental factors. This positioning depersonalizes

- As a result, what are similar organizations facing and finding out?
- What has been done or is planned by them to address those challenges?

the request and sets the tone that the request is aimed at overall organizational benefit.

Base the material on well-known facts, thus establishing a neutral frame of reference. Support your case with published articles or statistics.

If possible (confidentiality and competitive intelligence concerns may stand in the way), provide answers to questions about other organizations. Be sure that the organizations chosen for the environmental analysis are representative of your situation, specifically in terms of size and complexity.

What was the nature of the problem to be resolved, or the opportunity acted on?

What approach was taken? What were the key features of the project?

What were the project outcomes?

What benefits were achieved?

What were the project costs?

How long did it take to implement?

What were the critical success factors?

What were the lessons learned?

What, if anything, would be done differently next time?

Internal Analogies

- What other departments or groups within your organization are experiencing similar PNOs?

Base the material on discussions with contacts who perform similar functions in other departments and who have either resolved problems like your own or have pursued a comparable opportunity.

4. Options: Pros and Cons

Nature of this segment: A description of the options you believe are appropriate, among the universe of potential options.

Key Points to Include	Comments and Examples
• The *range* of options available to address the problem, need, or opportunity • The reasons why some have been eliminated as viable alternatives (at least for now)	Some organizations will require you to identify and consider alternative solutions and show how they will not work as well as the approach you are ultimately recommending. First address these questions: *What are the consequences of the "status quo" as an option?* *What are possible alternatives in addressing the PNO?* *What are some circumstances, costs, consequences, or other attributes that make some of the options less appropriate or workable?*
• A description of the remaining viable options that will address the PNO, with a summary of key features and their pros/cons	Then focus on two or three *viable* options. For *each* of the options you consider viable, explain: *What are its key features?* *What are the key benefits?* *What are the key drawbacks, risks, or constraints?*

5. Proposed Approach

Nature of this segment: A high-level description setting out how your proposed course of action will work in practice and how it will unfold.

Key Points to Include	Comments and Examples
• An opening statement of exactly what you want to do, and how you intend to go about it	Show that you have considered how each phase of the proposed course of action can be launched and achieved. While this segment is not a project plan in the sense of a week-by-week activity

	schedule, it gives sufficient detail so that readers can "see" the activities unfolding. List what you want to do: *On the basis of the foregoing considerations, which of the options are you proposing as your approach?*
	Show how you intend to go about it: *What are the action steps?* *What resources will be needed?* *Does the approach take advantage of existing resources such as partnerships and shared service opportunities?* *What is the overall time frame?*
• A list of the objectives to be accomplished	Describe the anticipated outcome: *What will be the results of undertaking your proposal?*
• The scope	Scope the project by identifying what will be included and not included: *What client groups or departments will be involved? Who will not be involved?* *What types of activities or services are included in the approach? What is out of scope?* *Does the approach entail a trial period or a phased rollout?*
• The critical success factors	Comment on the critical success factors: *Whose cooperation will be essential?* *What technology must be in place?* *What facilities need to be available?* *What capabilities must be present or acquired to ensure the necessary tools and expertise?*

• The steps involved in implementing the proposal	Show what work is involved in each stage of the implementation process: *What are the steps and the timelines for each stage?*

6. Budget and Cost Analysis

Nature of this segment: An articulation of the costs the proposal will entail.

Key Points to Include	Comments and Examples
• A description of the anticipated direct and indirect costs, with budget estimates	Identify and calculate the direct costs to be incurred for: *Salaries and benefits* *Consulting fees* *Purchases or subscriptions* *Capital investments (e.g. new technology)* *Training* *Materials* *Any other element (e.g. travel)* Identify and calculate the indirect costs for: *Facilities* *IT services* *Other (e.g. HR involvement)*
• Implications for existing and future budgets	Link the costs of the proposal with the current budget or projected budget estimates: *What costs can be covered by diverting funds from the existing budget?* *What new funds are required? Over what period of time?* *What costs could be assumed by other cost centers?* *Could end-of-year or discretionary funds be directed to the project?*

• An indication of the staffing effort required (regardless whether it requires new staff)	Include information about existing staff and potential needs for new staff: *Who will be involved in the project? For what specific purposes and for what period of time? What would be the job description for any new hire(s)?*
• [If relevant] Implications for current activities	If existing activities need to be temporarily limited or suspended, explain the situation: *At a funding level of A, all existing services will be maintained. At a funding level of B, some resources could be temporarily or permanently diverted to the project, resulting in such changes as ... At a funding level of C, the following activities will be terminated in favor of the proposed new ones ...*

7. Benefits

Nature of this segment: A detailed listing of the gains for the organization, from major impacts through ancillary and downstream benefits.

Key Points to Include	**Comments and Examples**
• The key benefits of the approach • How the proposal will address identified challenges	Quantify as many benefits as possible: *Who will benefit from the approach? (Specific client teams or groups, certain categories of jobs, etc.) Will the proposal save employee time? What are the estimated savings? Will the proposal maximize productivity on the part of beneficiaries? What are the estimated savings? Will it save dollars currently being spent on other products, services or technology? If so, what are the estimated savings?*

	Will the approach help avoid the expense of other costly approaches?
• Return on investment (ROI can be included in the Budget and Cost Analysis segment or in the Benefits segment)	The return on investment (ROI) compares the costs of the project with some measurement of its benefit (return). The math is challenging for nonprofit centers such as libraries to calculate, but where possible, try to obtain and use internal statistics that demonstrate contribution to the bottom line.
	Where internal statistics are not available, refer to the information gathered for the environmental analysis segment of your business case. Here is an example of how a productivity ROI is calculated:
	The price of the liberated time that can be directed to priority work = number of employees affected x number of hours saved weekly x number of average weeks worked x average hourly wage
	Identify non-quantifiable benefits as well:
	Will the proposal contribute to more informed and timely decision making? For what groups and specifically in what way?
	Will the proposal contribute to organizational competitive intelligence efforts?
	To what extent will it leverage investments in technology or information products?
	[etc.]

8. Strategic Alignment and Risk Mitigation

Nature of this segment: An assurance that the proposed course of action is well within the organization's culture and strategic direction.

Key Points to Include	Comments and Examples
• How the project aligns with and supports the overall business strategy of the organization	Show that you understand the strategic goals of your organization by quoting from official statements such as strategic priority or mission statements, annual reports, and executive presentations. Be sure to address such questions as: *How does your proposal align with the organization's **stated strategic priorities**?* *What departments or groups will be most impacted by your project? In what way?* *What period of time is envisioned for the project to be achieved? How does that time period match with the organization's overall strategic horizons?* *What other **initiatives** in your organization or in other specific departments will be impacted by your proposal? In what way?*
• Pre-emptive information to overcome immediate concerns (a.k.a. "I already thought of that")	What information can you serve up to deal with anticipated opposition? *What valid objections would likely be raised?* *What strategies will you employ to mitigate any negative impacts?* *How will the benefits of your approach outweigh any perceived disadvantages?*

9. Readiness to Proceed

Nature of this segment: Assurance that key enablers are in place and that there are no major barriers to proceeding other than what you are requesting.

Key Points to Include	Comments and Examples
• What has been done to date to ensure readiness • A statement of immediate next steps (upon approval)	First summarize and be specific about what you already have in place to move forward: *What has been done to date (without direct cost), or what is already in place so that the proposed course of action can be set in motion?* *What resources are available and ready to undertake the project?* *What are the immediate next steps, assuming approval?*
• A direct request for explicit authorization to proceed with the project and for the associated funding	Then state succinctly what stands between you and the project's start, and indicate any cautions: *What precisely do you require at this stage to put the project in motion? People? Funds? Facilities? Equipment?* *Is there a deadline for approval and project kickoff? If so, what are the reasons for the deadline? What would happen if that deadline were missed?*

10. Appendices

Nature of this segment: Supporting information deemed too detailed for the body of the case, yet still providing data or background that could be helpful for some readers.

Key Points to Include	Comments and Examples
• Documents, lists, tables, statistics, activity reports, and the like to orient the reader in support of your proposal, and substantiate the points made in it	Examples of items to append include: *Copies of previous studies or reports that relate to the situation being addressed* *Trend information internal to the organization (counts, measures, indicators)* *Trend information for the relevant industry, market, sector, etc.* *List of contacts consulted* *List of organizations following a similar approach* *Relevant articles from your literature search*

What's Next?

The next chapter discusses a template, adapted from the framework, with prompts to create a *brief* business case memorandum when organizational culture demands brevity.

CHAPTER 5

The Business Case Memorandum

In some instances, and depending on the organizational culture, a brief proposal in the form of a three- to four-page memorandum may be the most effective format in which to make your proposal.

Such a memorandum could simply be the tool by which you generate sufficient interest in your idea so that you are requested to prepare a full business case document. With luck, your culture may support a reaction such as "looks good—go for it!" If you are unsure what the culture supports, a trial memorandum cannot hurt (e.g., "If you would like a fuller document, I will be pleased to present one.").

Even though your memorandum may not include all the potential components found in the *Business Case Framework*, you will need to be prepared to answer additional questions, such as "Why didn't you choose to …?" or "What are other organizations doing about …?" What is written in the brief memo is only the foundation for further presentations you are likely to make.

Following are guidelines for the type of information to put into a memo format proposal. If you have additional content that makes a compelling case, be sure to include it as an attachment. The number of paragraphs for each topic is a suggestion only.

Business Case Memorandum Structure

To start the memorandum, use:

To:
From:
Date:
Re: Proposal for …

Paragraph 1: Three Bullets

- **Theme:** Identify the solution or opportunity to be discussed. The essence of what your proposal is selling—if possible, in a single statement.

- **Statement of Proposal:** Precisely articulate what you are proposing to do. Add detail later.

- **Result:** Highlight the outcome and the key benefit to be achieved if your proposal gets approved and implemented. Connect it to an organizational strategic goal (the distinction between "you get" and "I propose").

Paragraphs 2–3

- **Drivers:** Summarize the PNO with a note on its cause or history. Include the larger context in terms of the organization or the wider environment. If other solutions have been attempted or considered in the past, note briefly that they proved inappropriate and why.

Paragraphs 4–5

- **Options and Further Description:** Show options considered—and pros and cons—before zeroing in on the recommended option. Provide information about the scope of effort: who will be involved in the work, who will be impacted, when implementation is slated to occur, and what ramifications that timing may have.

Paragraph 6

- **Benefits:** Show a list of benefits related to the PNO shown in Paragraph 2.

Paragraphs 7–8

- **Costs and Support:** Include direct and indirect costs—consultant fees, license fees, staff salaries, facilities, equipment, travel, materials, etc. Indicate what support is needed from other departments such as IT and HR.

Paragraph 9

- **Approval**: Make a clear call to action, requesting authorization to begin the project.

Business Case Memorandum Illustration

The following is an example of a completed business case memorandum:

Title of Proposed Project **To:** **From:** **Date:** With this memo, I hereby request an opportunity to present a business case in person or via a formal business case document.	
Motivation, Proposal, and Benefits	**Motivated by** [problem, challenge, immediate need], we have the **opportunity** to [address it, take advantage of other events, ...] This memo is a **proposal** to [set up, establish, ...] **Business achievements** are expected to include [problem relief, competitive advantage, cost savings, ...]
Drivers and Options	The opportunity has arisen because ... I considered the following options and selected the one with the most relevant benefits ...
Recommended Approach	I plan to ... I can implement [when, how] I will need [individuals, groups, departments or resources, products, services]
Benefits	I considered other options and chose the recommended approach because it has the following benefits:

	A. Top Benefit B. Next Benefit C. Next Benefit
Costs and Support	Direct costs are estimated to be … Indirect costs include … In addition, we need assistance from … *The net new investment is …*
Approval	I am seeking authorization to proceed with the proposal and need approval for an expenditure of *X*.

What's Next?

The next chapter provides illustrations of three business cases, each reflecting aspects of the foregoing chapters.

CHAPTER 6

Case Studies

Author's note: These case studies are constructed from experience over several decades. They do not describe actual individuals, organizations, vendors, or financial amounts.

Case Study 1: Anne's Proposal to Hire an External Consultant

Background on Anne's Situation

Anne is the Manager of Library Services at Retired Employees Pension Service (REPS). In this independent corporation employing several hundred staff, approximately 200 knowledge workers—analysts, economists, actuaries, and many other types of professionals—are responsible for setting and implementing investment strategies for the pensions of large numbers of employees in a variety of funds.

REPS's priorities are evolving rapidly, and its key goals are creating challenges as well as opportunities for the Library Services group. Several new priorities relate to broadening the pension funds' asset mix, developing more actively managed investment strategies, and increasing investment in global markets. Other initiatives in the works are responding to new government policies with an impact on pension funds. All this movement is creating a demand—and an opportunity—for new information resources and practices.

On several occasions, Anne has raised with her immediate manager, the VP of Corporate Services, the possibility of undertaking an **information audit** that will provide input on the perceived value and use of the library's current information resources and practices, and help identify evolving information needs resulting from the changes her organization is experiencing. The VP has indicated his support in principle for the initiative.

Anne and two of her four staff are prepared to conduct a high-level assessment of the *usage* of existing information assets, but she understands the **benefits of hiring an external consultant** to undertake the **user needs** assessment portion of the audit. The VP has asked her to put together a business case for undertaking the audit and specifically for hiring an external consultant; he will then take the case to the Executive Committee. Prompted by the VP's query about the meaning of the term "audit," Anne has decided to term her initiative an "information use study" in order to defuse any negative connotations "audit" might have among employees.

Although Anne's business case is focused on the authorization to hire an external consultant for the user needs assessment, she also wants to **lay the groundwork** for the later implementation of the consultant's findings. She knows the business case for the consultant is only the beginning of what will be a significant strategic project to tailor information services to changing needs.

Anne has **looked into information audits for some time**. By attending a library conference workshop, she was able to identify an information audit as the best process for addressing the challenges her library is experiencing and for shedding light on the opportunities it has to support knowledge workers in the challenging times ahead. She used the bibliography she received at the workshop to do further reading and has communicated with several library colleagues to get their advice and experience in undertaking comparable projects and in hiring an external consultant. She incorporates a record of her preparation into the business case to ensure it is clear she is requesting approval for a well-known process.

Anne's Adaptation of the Framework

In this case study, we see how Anne starts working on her business case by noting the data and key points she wants to include in each of the sections of the *Business Case Framework*. As she works through the process, she adapts the framework to her specific needs.

As she reviews her key points, Anne highlights those she believes should be incorporated into the one-page Executive Summary.

Given the fast-paced environment in which she works, and the number of items on upcoming Executive Committee agendas, Anne plans on a document no longer than five pages. To provide a bit more depth, she adds an Appendix containing an overview of options considered.

What's Next?

We cover Anne's building blocks, illustrated vis-à-vis the *framework*. Explanatory commentary (not included in Anne's actual document but intended to give a rationale for Anne's choices) is shown with a shaded background.

Author's note regarding the level of detail in Anne's document: The corporate culture in Anne's organization dictates a high-level, key-points-only, bullet style for proposals. Contrast such a culture with that of Michael's in Case Study 3 where a detailed narrative is called for.

Proposal to Hire an External Consultant to Assist with an Information Use Study

Anne's Executive Summary

Anne anticipates using the *Executive Summary* as the basis for a memo she will send to her manager in preparation for a briefing meeting about her proposal.	
Anne's Key Points	**Comments**
<ul><li>What is proposed</li><li>The drivers for the proposal</li><li>The effort and investment</li><li>Key benefits to be realized</li></ul>	After noting points she wants to include in the body of her proposal, Anne goes back and **highlights** the key points to include in the Executive Summary. Her Executive Summary, therefore, will consist of concise statements condensed from the text of the proposal. That way, she achieves "recognition" on the part of the reader when points already made in the Executive Summary are encountered in the body.

Anne's Background and Strategic Alignment Segment

Anne decides to combine the sections on *Background* and *Strategic Alignment*. The drivers for her initiative are so connected to new organization wide strategic directions that she believes it is important to present them together.

Anne's Key Points	Anne's Notes (to be featured in her memo)
Background: • What the problem, need, or opportunity is	The library's information resources and environmental scanning practices (responsibility of the library and another group within Corporate Services) are **not meeting the information needs of the Executive team and clients in the Investment and Policy departments**.
• Evidence of the PNO	The evidence is that the library is receiving an increasing number of requests for resources and information that it does not hold or has not licensed. Library staff are hearing more and more employees complain about **frustration in the amount of time they are spending in information seeking, but the Library doesn't have documentation on specific needs or gaps**.
• How the PNO originated	A 30 percent year-over-year decline during the last three years in requests for existing resources suggests that those resources, while they may have been needed in the past, are not suitable for evolving needs.

• The current situation	At library orientation sessions for new employees, **new hires are identifying resources, not available here, to which they had access in their previous workplaces.** Library staff note considerable differences in information seeking practices between new (and younger) hires and long-term employees. A mini client satisfaction survey for the Library's *Media Update* showed **enthusiastic support for more timely and customized current awareness from a single source within the organization.**
Indication of how the project aligns with the overall business strategy of the organization: • The opportunity at hand • The potential impact of the opportunity on the organization • How it may impact other initiatives and stakeholders	**The opportunity to explore and understand more about our key clients' evolving information related needs, preferences, and practices will allow us to acquire and design new library products and services that match specialized needs, thus directing budget resources to priority content and efforts.** **Areas with information gaps correlate directly to our new investment strategies.** As well, the recent current-awareness survey indicated the need to monitor for information about public firms in our industry, corporate governance, and federal government policy initiatives.

Anne's Options Segment

Anne omits the section *Environmental Analysis* and goes next to *Options* because one of the benefits she notes in her rationale for hiring an external consultant is that the consultant will contribute to the knowledge of what is happening in similar organizations. Anne will seek to learn, through the consultant, about the approaches other organizations have taken in similar situations, and what the associated benefits, costs, implementation time, and critical success factors were.

Anne's Key Points	Anne's Notes (to be featured in her memo)
• The *range* of options available to address the problem, need, or opportunity	The Information Use Study will have three key components: 1. Review of the current information assets' utility. 2. Examination of client information needs. 3. Gap analysis: What is missing? Range of options for the study: 1. Status quo. 2. Library staff conduct all aspects of the Information Use Study. 3. Hire an external consultant to conduct a survey of client information needs and use. Library staff conduct a review of the current use of information assets. 4. Hire an external consultant to conduct all aspects of the Information Use Study.
• The rationale as to why some have been eliminated as non-viable alternatives	Non-viable options: 1. Status Quo: "Doing nothing" to redefine Library resources and services is not an option given the pace of change at REPS and the

	perceived inadequacy of existing information resources. 2. Library staff will undertake the study. Although they are knowledgeable and have the benefit of familiarity with REPS, they are without the benefit of insight into other organizations' approaches and are not experienced in the process of an information audit.
• A description of the remaining viable options and a summary of their pros/cons	Viable options considered: 1. Hire an external consultant to conduct a survey of client information needs and use. Library staff conduct a review of information assets' current use. 2. Hire an external consultant to conduct all aspects of the Information Use Study.

Pros and Cons:
Anne creates a simple matrix to summarize the key features, benefits, and constraints of each of the two viable options. She decides to include the matrix as an Appendix.

Anne's Proposed Approach Segment

Anne's Key Points	Anne's Notes (to be featured in her memo)
• An opening statement of the recommended option	**Preferred Option:** **The Library is seeking authorization and funding to hire an external consultant to examine REPS knowledge workers' current and likely future information needs. As**

part of the project, Library staff will work closely with the consultant and will conduct a high-level review of the use presently being made of the Library's information assets.

• A list of the objectives to be accomplished by following this option

Objectives: By working with an outside expert, we will ...

1. Acquire unbiased in-depth knowledge about REPS knowledge workers' information needs, use, and any current access barriers they perceive— focusing not only on *what* information is required but on *how* and *for what purposes* information is needed.

2. Learn about REPS knowledge workers' preferences regarding access and format.

3. Benefit from "lessons learned" through the consultant's knowledge of organizations similar to our own.

Meeting these objectives means that Library Services will have taken an important first step in being able to offer the kind of information services that are critical for REPS to create sound investment strategies, timely responses to government and private initiatives, and a proactive policy development to set the standard for our industry.

• The scope

Scope:
The study will include all members of the Executive Committee, selected Board members, and representatives from Corporate Services and Investment and Policy groups. The study will consider information processes as well as content.

The assessment of usage of Library information assets will include externally acquired information as well as information products produced in-house by the Library (e.g., Key Web Links on the intranet).

- The critical success factors

Critical success factors:
- Executive Committee's commitment for all members to meet individually with consultant to offer their personal vision and interests regarding information access.
- Executive Committee's active support to ensure participation in the study by others.
- Executive Committee's acknowledgement that the study is a first step in a longer-term project. Without a commitment to implementation of at least some of the recommendations flowing from the consultant's survey, there could be untoward consequences (if expectations arise and then are not met).

- The steps to undertake in implementing the proposal

Work steps have been planned for a 12-week time line:
Weeks 1–2: Library Services Manager (LSM) will prepare an RFP. Upon approval, it will be sent to 4 information management consultants (already known to LSM).

Library staff meet to plan and assign responsibility for high-level usage assessment; it should be completed in time to be used by the consultant for orientation.

	Weeks 3–5: LSM and staff review responses to RFP and select consultants to be interviewed.
	Week 6: LSM and VP Corporate Services select a consultant. LSM and Library staff meet with selected consultant to discuss and plan the study approach.
	Weeks 7–12: LSM works closely with consultant throughout the execution of the study and the crafting of the project report.

Anne's Budget and Cost Analysis Segment

Anne's Key Points	**Anne's Notes (to be featured in her memo)**
• A description of the direct and indirect costs that will be incurred, with budget estimates	**Direct Costs:** 1. **Estimated fee for consultant to undertake user information needs assessment is $30,000.** This fee cannot be covered by the Library budget. The fee will permit: (1) individual interviews with all Executive Committee members, selected Board members, selected knowledge workers, and (2) focus group meetings with several groups in the Investment, Policy, and Corporate Services units. 2. Attendance at an Information Audit workshop for two Library staff members is $1,000—to be paid from the Library's Professional

	Development/Conferences budget envelope.
• An indication of the staff effort required	**Indirect Costs:** 1. **Library staff time. All staff will be involved in various ways.** In addition to staff involvement identified in *Proposed Approach*, Library staff will schedule interviews and focus group participation, book meeting rooms, arrange refreshments, etc. 2. **REPS staff time to participate in some of the interviews and focus group meetings** (anticipate approximately 1 hour per interview and 1.5 hours per focus group event).

Anne's Benefits Segment

In this section, Anne focuses on the paybacks of hiring an external consultant. She does touch on the long-term benefits but does not attempt to quantify them at this stage; she believes such quantification will be part of the business plan she ultimately will develop when the recommendations from the Information Use Study are to be implemented.

Anne's Key Points	Anne's Notes (to be featured in her memo)
• What the principal benefits of the approach are	**Main Benefit:** **Hiring an external consultant will enable us to obtain candid observations and insights into the "information way of life" of our Executive team and of REPS knowledge workers, thus identifying their true requirements.**

• How the proposal will address the challenges already identified	Knowing what is truly needed will allow us to plan how to tailor content and services much more closely to actual needs, thus supporting key individuals' productivity and contribution toward REPS goals.
• Timeframe for benefits to manifest	The anticipated timeframe for benefits to become tangible for REPS employees is estimated at a modest 6 months.
• Return on investment	**Return on Investment:** The Information Use Study is the first step in a larger project to align information resources with the work of REPS' business units. The indicators of lack of alignment between existing information assets and work assignments were identified in the *Background* section. The consultant's recommendations will point to strategies and concrete actions we can undertake to correct the underlying disconnects.

Anne's Readiness to Proceed Segment

Anne's Key Points	Anne's Notes (to be featured in her memo)
• What has been done to date	**Preparatory steps have been completed so that the Library is ready to proceed with issuing an RFP, selecting a consultant, and guiding the consultant as the study is launched.**

	The Library Manager has consulted with other librarians about similar projects, with Library staff, and with the VP, Corporate Services.
	The Library Manager has identified suitable consultants.
• A specific request for authorization to proceed with the project	The Library is seeking approval to issue an RFP that will be sent to four external information management consultants. A sum of $30,000 is required for allocation to this part of the Information Use Study.
• A statement of immediate next steps	Immediate next steps: 1. Meet with Library staff for input on RFP. 2. Prepare a draft RFP for review by the VP, Corporate Services. 3. Send an electronic version of the RFP to four information management consultants. Copies also go to Corporate Services, HR, and Finance.

Anne's Appendix

Anne's Key Points	Comments
• Documents to support the proposal	If it is requested, Anne could include the results and recommendations that came out of her current awareness survey done earlier.

> In addition, she could consider referring to the fact that a similar project was recently undertaken at ABC Investments.
>
> Finally, she could consider including summaries of articles on information audits by leading library experts.

The Option Matrix Anne Presents in the Appendix

Option	Pros/Cons	Considerations
Do nothing.	Gap between Library offerings and knowledge worker needs will widen, increasing the amount of wasted time and employee dissatisfaction.	Not an attractive scenario for REPS at this crucial time.
Library staff conduct all aspects of the Information Use Study.	No out of pocket cost. Familiarity with REPS' culture, history, and key stakeholders. Potential lack of impartiality in responses. The Library enjoys a very favorable reputation in our organization, but we need to see the true picture of information needs,	If staff undertake all aspects of the study, some existing services to clients will be delayed. Staff have no previous experience in the design of information audits.

	practices, gaps, etc., without extraneous concerns about being tactful on the part of participants in the study.	
Recommended		
Hire an external consultant to conduct a survey of client information needs and use. Library staff will conduct a high level review of information assets' current use.	Will bring an impartial view and will be able to solicit "how it is" input (rather than "what they think we want to hear as they do not wish to criticize Library staff"). Opportunity for us to learn about best practices, as the consultant will have knowledge of other organizations, including their information-related challenges and solutions. Consultants have expertise and experience we do not have in the design of interview instruments and conducting focus group discussions.	Upfront costs are lessened through the involvement of Library staff in some aspects of the study. Also, we can tailor costs by varying the number of individual interviews and meetings. Consultants are not familiar with REPS' culture, history, and key stakeholders. Library staff will need to provide the necessary context.

	Hiring an external consultant lends credibility and "clout" to the project. Library staff will still be highly involved and visible.	

▲   ▲   ▲   ▲   ▲   ▲   ▲

Case Study 2: Kim's Options in a Proposal for Hiring a Librarian and Licensing Key Scientific Content

Background on Kim's Situation

Kim is the Director of Community Outreach at the Wellness Lifestyle Foundation, a small philanthropy funded organization focusing on disseminating information to communities interested in health promotion and protection through optimal nutrition and lifestyle—from individuals to health care providers to social workers to policy makers. In recent years, it has become clear that the science, public health, and sociology analysts are spending a lot of time keeping up to date in their fields by searching for articles and reports dealing with medical aspects, nutrition and exercise, herbal supplements and alternative therapies, economic impacts, health promotion strategies, etc.

All in all, Kim is convinced the organization, though it is small, is ready for a formal information supply strategy for the analysts. Here's why: It is particularly noticeable that analysts are amassing voluminous personal collections of article copies. Further probing reveals that each keeps a personal database of references to published articles, and that across the 35 analysts, duplication is frequent. The appearance of multiple copies of the same report suggests analysts have no way to determine what is already on hand in the organization. There are print subscriptions to 20 major journals considered relevant, but individual issues tend to get lost even though they are supposed to be passed from one reader to the next and then stored in a small reading area.

Each analyst uses a personal array of sources and methods including professional relationships with colleagues in similar organizations, visits to a large local holistic health bookstore, the city's public library, and—especially—searches in various free Web-based services. It has come to Kim's attention that the **analysts appear to miss key information** available only in specialized for-fee resources and that, at times, they miss material available in the free resources because they have not received formal instruction in search methods.

Finally, Kim has learned that many of the analysts are **not fully up to date** on developments in the relevant fields because they do not have access to current awareness services that would alert them to new publications and news about relevant conferences and political and policy developments. Although the small size of the organization makes for effective "water cooler" information exchange, it worries Kim that analysts may be working without the benefit of being able to shape their work according to the latest information. There are risks that some work is being done unnecessarily and some opportunities are being lost or belatedly leveraged because analysts are not aware that other organizations have already performed similar research or are currently launching initiatives to which the Wellness Lifestyle Foundation should be party.

Out of a small discretionary budget line, Kim engages a consultant specializing in health-related information research to help develop for the executive team a business case for (1) hiring a research professional, and (2) obtaining licenses to key relevant content. Kim outlines the current challenges in terms of two key exposures:

- Missed information: Risk of error, embarrassment, and lost opportunities

- Wasted time: Degreed experts are spending (duplicated) time at basic search efforts

Options: Recognizing that it may be a stretch, both conceptually and in terms of the investment, for the executive team to accept a proposal for a full-time research professional and for the full gamut of relevant content, Kim sets out a matrix of options illustrating several choices and their associated costs and ramifications. In so doing, Kim also makes the point that a phased approach could be considered; for example, in the first year the basic options could be funded as the organization gears up for larger investments in years 2 and 3.

Generic language: Deliberately, Kim keeps the language generic and to some extent simplifies the ramifications for the sake of clarity. The consultant has provided a "shopping list" with the names and known costs of commercial information products, details on the license terms (single or multiple users), and other contract details familiar to information professionals. Such details are needed when it comes to negotiating with vendors, but they are irrelevant for executives who are not familiar with the information industry. Similarly, various combinations of the six option scenarios will produce many different outcomes, but Kim's objective is to obtain approval for a spending envelope that will then be allocated for the most value. What the decision makers need is a clear picture that *increased investment will produce increased value for the organization and thus for its stakeholders.*

What's Next?

We cover Kim's options matrix.

Author's note regarding the level of detail in Kim's document: The corporate culture in Kim's organization dictates a succinct presentation.

Research Options: Basic to Ideal Support for Knowledge Workers

Professional Librarian

With respect to the services of an information professional, options include using a freelance researcher on demand, hiring a part-time librarian, and hiring a full-time librarian.

Note on the cost/benefit: Analysts indicate that they each require access to external scholarly/news information approximately 15 times per year. A freelance searcher's average charge per search would be in the $400 range, for a total outsourced cost of $210,000. Such an expense compares unfavorably with the cost of a full-time librarian, as shown.

	$ per year	**Ramifications**
Basic Freelance researcher (1 day/week)	$25,000	At 1 day per week, the contractor can provide slightly less than 400 hours, equaling 10 hours per analyst per year—inadequate according to the analyst's stated needs.
Intermediate Part-time librarian (2–3 days/week)	$45,000	At 2 days per week, the librarian can divide 770 hours among searches and current awareness packages—22 hours per analyst per year.
	$65,000	At 3 days a week: 33 hours per analyst per year.
Ideal Full-time librarian	$100,000	The librarian can develop full service range of on-demand research, current awareness monitoring for groups and individuals, briefing summaries for executives, assistance with preparation of material for distribution to target audiences, and more.

Content Licensing

The proposed licenses to for-fee content have been grouped into tiers according to the consultant's recommendations:

- Tier 1 represents must-have resources covering the essential journals in nutrition, holistic health, and related public policy.

- Tier 2 encompasses resources covering a larger base of the world's scientific and professional publishing.

- Tier 3 contains specialized sources in the area of biomedical research as well as relevant media coverage in the world's major newspapers and magazines.

Note on savings offset: WLF currently spends a little more than $70,000 per year on the purchase of article copies (100 articles per analyst) and $10,000 on journal subscriptions. That $80,000 expense would be partially or fully saved by each content licensing option. A cancellation of all subscriptions is assumed here.

	$ per Year	Ramifications
Basic Tier 1	$50,000 Reduction in current $80,000 article purchase cost: $40,000 **Net new investment:** **$10,000**	• Access to mainstream scholarly publications. • No access to media coverage. • For comprehensive access to scholarly material, an estimated 2,000 needed articles, not available in Tier 1, would still be purchased ad hoc at $20, equaling $40,000.
Intermediate Tiers 1 + 2	$75,000 Reduction in current $80,000 article purchase cost: $60,000 **Net new investment:** **$15,000**	• Access to a wider scope of scholarly publications. • No access to media coverage. • An estimated 1,000 needed articles, not available in Tiers 1 and 2, must still be purchased ad hoc at $20, equaling $20,000.
Ideal Tiers 1 + 2 + 3	$100,000 Reduction in current $80,000 article purchase cost: $80,000 **Net new investment:** **$20,000**	• Comprehensive access to scholarly publications, biomedical research, and media coverage. • Insignificant additional ad hoc purchases.

Although the recommended approach would be a combination of the two **ideal** options, other combinations could be considered. For example:

Net New Investment Range	Librarian Option	Content Option
$120,000	Ideal	Ideal
$ 80,000	Intermediate (3 days/wk)	Ideal
$ 60,000	Intermediate (2 days/wk)	Intermediate
$ 35,000	Basic	Basic

▲　　▲　　▲　　▲　　▲　　▲　　▲

Case Study 3: Michael's Proposal for Licensing a News Monitoring Service

Background on Michael's Situation

Michael is the Manager of the Information Resource Center (IRC) at Taylor Twynne, a professional services company focusing on six major industry groups including government services. The company is growing: Media & Entertainment (M&E) was added recently to its roster of industry practice groups, bringing the total number of employees to about 300. As well, the company is expanding its global business. As a result, reorganization has led to new hiring and realigning of personnel. Michael himself has been with the company for only a few months. He was hired by, and reports to, the new Director of Business Development.

The IRC employs three people in addition to Michael. Its current service mix includes reference and research services, current awareness services (*Taylor Twynne Today*), journal routing, document provision (an in-house collection and document delivery service), and management of internal Taylor Twynne documents.

Michael has taken the opportunity as a new employee to introduce himself to many of the company employees and to hold informal discussions about their information needs and practices.

Employees have traditionally received **one-size-fits-all services**, but recently the IRC has been offering extended service to the M&E practice group, whose members were very receptive to Michael's offer for the IRC to work more closely with them. An information professional on his staff attends the group's weekly meeting in which ongoing and new projects and clients are discussed. With this insight, Michael and his staff have been able to begin offering a limited "portfolio service" to the group.

The portfolio service—a term denoting dedicated offerings to a given target group—is a first step in what Michael sees as **a changing role for the IRC**. The IRC's clients are increasingly opting for more self-research, primarily searching Web sites at their desktops, but it is evident they need more and better content and tools. He has discussed two strategic goals with his manager: first, a shift toward an information management focus, with IRC personnel spending more time in identifying, acquiring, describing, organizing, and maintaining information resources; and second, a focus on identifying and working with key client groups to develop services targeted to their specific needs.

Michael's conversations with employees across the company, along with the input from the M&E group, have made it clear that the **greatest challenge is media monitoring** content and practices. He sees an opportunity to address the problem by **linking its solution with an enterprise portal development project** that has just been started in the company, thus creating an opening for the IRC to be part of the portal development team.

As a first step to delivering in-depth, personalized information resources and tools to the desktop, Michael has approached his manager, the Director of Business Development, about introducing a new media monitoring service. She is excited by Michael's vision but believes that his plan will best succeed if it is approached and launched as a relatively small pilot demonstration. Michael has suggested that the IRC start on a project basis with M&E. She has asked him to prepare a business case for the project to take to the senior management team, with the understanding that what he is proposing is a limited-scale project that will ultimately be followed by a service initiative for all employees. Thus the business case needs to have both short- and long-term perspectives.

What's Next?

Michael's written business case is presented.

Author's note regarding the Budget and Cost Analysis portion of Michael's business case: You will know from experience that it is very difficult to cost out new products and services until much discussion, comparison, and negotiation with vendors have taken place. If appropriate, your business case should clearly state how the costing is developed from best estimates and indications.

Michael's dollar figures are provided for illustration and should not be interpreted as vendor quotes. Many factors influence the final costs, and the vendor details have been omitted so as to give prominence to the justification and benefits.

Author's note regarding the level of detail in Michael's document: The corporate culture in Taylor Twynne dictates a high level of operational detail in proposals. Your own business case document may well be a fraction of the size of Michael's if your corporate culture calls for succinct proposals.

Proposal for a Pilot *Issues and Industry Intelligence Service* for Taylor Twynne

Table of Contents

1. Executive Summary

The IRC proposes a proof-of-concept to demonstrate the time savings and productivity gains for knowledge workers by investing in a leading-edge global and industry news service providing information and intelligence about Taylor Twynne's specialized industry sectors, competitors, customers, business partners, and sourcing prospects.

The proposal requests authorization to fund a *pilot demonstration* in the range of $25,000–30,000 for six months. The Director of M&E has indicated a willingness to contribute $10,000.

How will Taylor Twynne benefit from enhanced media monitoring?

- **Productivity gains:** A white paper prepared by a leading international research firm suggested years ago that knowledge workers spend much more time looking for information than might be assumed. We estimate that knowledge workers at Taylor Twynne currently spend 9.5 hours per week on information seeking, costing the company approximately $19,000 per worker per year. Saving 225 practice group Consultants and Administrative Assistants even two to three hours per week will result in a productivity savings of more than $1 million.

- **Performance advantage:** We are planning a service that has the potential to bring thousands of newswires, publications, transcripts, and company and industry reports from more than 100 countries to our employees' desktops. Taylor Twynne is known for its investment in hiring leading experts in its practice fields—we hereby give the experts the expert tools.

- **Cost per user compares favorably to costs for other corporate services:** The cost per user for the prototype service is estimated to be $300 per month. Average total monthly cell phone and PDA communication costs per employee (as reported for the last fiscal year) were in excess of this amount.

- **Leveraging technology investments:** The *Issues and Industry Intelligence Service* will maximize the planned investment in portal software. Now is the right time to leverage the investment because the two efforts will achieve synergy.

- **Competitive advantage:** Not only will the new service enable top performance on the part of analysts, it will also contribute to our ability to attract and retain top talent, thus maximizing our return on the considerable investment we make in our analysts.

Why is the proposed new service needed? Because right now, it is a pressing problem that:

- Employees are forced to spend too much time looking for relevant news. They have to search in too many locations for news that is buried in the inconsistently organized corporate intranet.

- Global or industry news is not available as needed.

- There is some duplication in purchase of information and in effort by two groups: the IRC and Corporate Communications.

- Employees are unable to access media monitoring services at all when they are away from their desktops.

Why proceed now?

- The expansion of our business into new global and industry markets creates demand for more global and industry information.

- The opportunity to leverage the enterprise portal initiative is a strategic gain.

- The current collaboration between the IRC and M&E will serve as a strong starting point for the project.

What are the options?

We present two viable options for delivering a robust news service to Taylor Twynne employees. The **preferred** option is for the IRC to work with M&E to create a new *Issues and Industry Intelligence Service* prototype. The IRC and the Corporate Communications group will continue to supply existing media monitoring services to all other company employees for the short term.

Industry content selected for the prototype relates to the media, broadcasting, and entertainment industries. News content to be tested is broader in scope, covering selected local, regional, national, and global sources.

The project will begin as soon as approval is received. Results will be reported six weeks after the end of the six-month project.

The project should be seen as the first step in the provision of an extended media monitoring service to all knowledge workers at Taylor Twynne.

What will it cost?

- The prototype project will incur costs for a trial subscription to a major global and industry news service.

- For the purposes of the pilot project, we have selected a news and industry package with a range of monitoring capabilities; it does not require integration into our corporate intranet for us to get started.

- Based on discussions with other librarians and preliminary and informal discussion with the content vendor, the content cost for the prototype is estimated to be $25,000–30,000 for six months.

- The prototype project will require no new staffing.

- There is no room in the current library budget to purchase additional news content. However, the Director of the M&E practice group has indicated a willingness to divert $10,000 from current subscriptions in his department to the project.

2. Background

Industry practice group employees at Taylor Twynne need access to a global and industry news service so they can obtain information and intelligence about our specialized industry sectors, competitors, customers, business partners, and sourcing prospects.

Employees do not currently have access to such a service. The IRC proposes to begin work on delivering a service that:

- Combines news from a wide variety of media with in-depth industry information on issues and trends.

- Integrates content from external media products with content from other information resources key to our business (e.g., government and industry association Web sites).

- Integrates external content with internal information for "one-stop information shopping."

- Is constantly updated.

- Sits on the desktop of every knowledge worker at Taylor Twynne.

- Can be customized to specific groups and personalized for individuals.

- Can be accessed via PDAs.

- Is automated and straightforward to maintain, with a set of flexible administrative tools.

Current Media Monitoring Situation

Media monitoring is currently the responsibility of two groups in the company.

The **IRC** monitors the major national and regional news sources, subscribing to three separate services. Users go to the IRC's page on the intranet to select stories from topical folders. One IRC staff person devotes approximately 50 percent of her time to administering the service. All employees have access to *Taylor Twynne Today*, updated early each business day.

Corporate Communications subscribes to a large external media monitoring service that supplies the content for a daily service prepared for Corporate Services personnel and senior management. This service, *Taylor Twynne in the News*, refers to mentions of TT in traditional news and broadcast media outlets, as well as the Internet, and is delivered via email throughout the day, based on a user-determined frequency. Corporate Communications in addition prepares a weekly summary, *Taylor Twynne Week in Review*, for all employees and posts it each Friday to the company intranet. Corporate Communications devotes one full-time staff person to administering the media monitoring service. This employee reports increasing costs and some concerns about the external service.

Limitations in Current Media Monitoring

Several factors indicate that a new approach to media monitoring is called for:

- **There is duplication in purchase of information and in effort:** Some of the same news content is being purchased twice—once by the IRC and again as part of Corporate Communications' service. Similarly, efforts and processes are being duplicated, particularly as they relate to *Taylor Twynne Week in Review*.

- **Employees are forced to spend too much time looking for relevant news:** There are many industries, issues, and interests to track, especially as our company expands and becomes more global. The result is (1) the creation of more and more topical folders in which the IRC organizes the news, and (2) a large number of news items being added to the folders on a daily basis. But employees need to be able to find quickly the few items matching their specific interests each day. We require tools to deliver only the news that is most relevant to each of our users—they do not have time to scan through pages and pages of news items. Currently, as a result of that challenge, some employees are relying on a single Web-based source; therefore, they miss important items that are reported in alternate news sources.

- **At the same time, there is insufficient global or industry content in the news we do get:** Information resources have not kept up with new business practices at Taylor Twynne. This is particularly true in the case of global and industry news. Currently, many of our consultants are relying on a patchwork of personal contacts, public industry Web sites, hardcopy journal subscriptions, and research done by the IRC. They need access to more industry information at their desktops. (Appendix 1 compares a list of key industry journals for media, broadcasting, and entertainment with a list of those available electronically on the desktops of M&E.)

- **Employees are missing important information:** The IRC's intranet homepage—where news folders are displayed—is two levels below the corporate intranet homepage. We have recently learned that some employees are not even aware that *Taylor Twynne Today* exists. We have now put in place a new-employee IRC orientation program that will help rectify this situation, but a daily news service should be "front and center" on each desktop.

- **Lack of consistency leads to confusion:** The Corporate Communications group and the IRC use different classification systems for organizing information, leading to confusion and waste of time.

- **From their desktops, employees cannot access news that is older than two weeks:** The maximum archival period for which news content is purchased is two weeks. For older items, employees must request assistance from the IRC.

- **Employees are unable to access media monitoring services at all when they are away from their desktops:** We need flexible methods for employees to receive information using mobile devices.

The Opportunity—Now

Several things have come together to make now an optimum time to introduce a new media-monitoring product:

- **Expansion of our business:** Growth at Taylor Twynne has created an urgent need for a better solution to track global and industry events.

- **New technology initiatives:** The company has created a Portal Planning Team to select and purchase enterprise portal software. The reasons to implement portal technology are in fact the same reasons for implementing a dynamic media monitoring service:

    - Different roles require different information (customization).

    - Different people with the same role work differently (personalization).

    - People need to get directly to the right information (work flow).

- **Collaboration:** Staff of the IRC have been working closely with M&E. This offers the basis, and an opportunity, for working closely together on a customized news service that will truly meet everyone's needs.

3. Options

Potential Options: Overview and Rationale

Options range from maintaining the status quo, i.e., a continuation of the existing media monitoring services, to the creation of an *Issues and Industry Intelligence Service* for all employees at Taylor Twynne. This service would deliver a wide range of news and information content to desktops and offer a full array of features and capabilities.

This business case has been prepared because continuation of the **status quo is not seen as a viable option**. As well, the media monitoring services as they exist cannot be altered and improved upon to a degree that makes the time, effort, and cost in doing so an efficient use of company resources.

Most importantly, delaying changes to media monitoring means a **lost opportunity for integration** with our enterprise portal implementation. Participation on and input to the Portal Planning Team at these early stages will result in a news service that is a dynamic component of our enterprise portal.

Planning and delivering a full *Issues and Industry Intelligence Service* to all company employees at the same time, and in the near future, is also being ruled out as a viable option. To do so would require extensive resources—staff time and expenditures for information content and technology. As well, given that the new portal software is currently at the planning and selection stage, it would be premature to implement a new content service across the company. A phased approach is therefore recommended.

Viable Options for Consideration

Option 1: Deliver a new media monitoring service with extended news content to *all* company employees. Industry information and content tools and features will be integrated when the portal development is completed.

Key Features	Benefits	Constraints
All employees will have access to much needed additional news coverage (particularly global). There will be a single service—existing overlap and duplication will be eliminated.	Enhanced ability to make informed decisions. Some cost savings in eliminating existing duplication in services. Employee time savings in reducing the number of places to look. Time savings for IRC and Corporate Communications staff in not maintaining the existing services.	There will be new costs to acquire additional content. Integration with company-wide portal software implementation will entail additional work. Two major initiatives will be under way back-to-back (news content *can* be delivered without integration into the corporate intranet—but that is not optimal).

Option 2: Continue the existing media monitoring services to all company employees for the short term but work with M&E on a prototype service.

Key Features	Benefits	Constraints
M&E staff will have access, on a trial basis, to a collection of news and industry resources that they have helped to identify and prioritize. Selection and access to the resources will be personalized to match their information "profiles." IRC staff will work with M&E, Corporate Communications, and IT staff as well as the information content vendor to deploy the trial service.	Offers an opportunity for staff (IRC, IT, Communications, Consultants) to learn and develop expertise with a small scale project. Fits well with the Portal Planning Team effort. Information content vendor is likely to offer some financial incentive to support a small-scale trial project that will lead to a later company-wide rollout. Feedback from M&E users will benefit later implementation of full service.	Majority of company employees will still have access to only the existing media monitoring services. IRC staff will have less time to monitor and "tweak" the existing service, so there may be some diminishment in *Taylor Twynne Today.* The prototype project will require time and commitment from staff in IRC, Corporate Communications, M&E, and IT.

4. Environmental Analysis

To conduct an environmental analysis, the IRC Manager:

- Met several times with the Manager, Corporate Communications.
- Contacted and spoke with the information professionals of three companies where significant investments in media monitoring have been made (see Appendix 2).
- Held preliminary discussions with two major information service vendors.

- Conducted a search of the literature for relevant articles on media monitoring services (see Appendix 3).

Key Findings
Approaches taken by other companies

- In all three companies, the information resource center is responsible for administering the media monitoring service.

- Two of the companies are using the content vendor selected for our prototype; one company is using the services of multiple content vendors and manually integrating the information into a proprietary company portal.

- One of the companies is using the full range of vendor content tools to integrate external information into employee workflow.

- All three companies started with a trial project before making the service available to large groups of employees.

Benefits

- All three information professionals indicated that their monitoring services had been enthusiastically received; evidence bears it out in that all three have expanded the service from what was originally conceived.

- The main benefit was time savings in seeking information and the resulting acceleration of the decision making cycle.

- It was noted that recipients expressed "feeling assured" they would not be caught short by missing important information.

Critical success factors

- Partnership with IT right from the initial stages.

- Selection of a service with features allowing easy integration into an intranet and configuration to users' needs.

- Selection of a vendor offering a consulting branch.

- An understanding that the role of the information resource center or library changes as employees increasingly use the service not only for "news" monitoring but for self-service research; job roles and responsibilities consequently all change.

- Sufficient information resource center staff to provide support to users, particularly at startup and for personalization.

5. Proposed Approach

The IRC proposes to work with M&E to introduce a new *Issues and Industry Intelligence Service* prototype. The IRC and Corporate Communications will continue to supply existing media monitoring services to all other company employees for the short term but see this project as the first step in providing a comprehensive media monitoring service to all knowledge workers at Taylor Twynne.

Objectives

At the conclusion of the prototype project, the following objectives will have been met:

1. M&E, working with IRC staff, will have identified, prioritized, selected, used, and evaluated industry information specific to their business needs.

2. IRC staff will have identified, prioritized, selected, and evaluated regional, national, and global news sources for ultimate use by all employees of Taylor Twynne.

3. IRC staff will have established a working relationship with a major information content provider.

4. IRC staff will have learned about, used, and offered instruction and assistance to the M&E group on tools that enable customization and personalization of the content acquired. This will lead to the development of training guidelines for all staff.

5. IRC staff will have a model to be used in working with other practice groups.

Scope

- Staff of the IRC, IT Department, Corporate Communications, and M&E practice will partner in the project.

- The IRC Manager will be the lead.

- Industry content selected for the prototype relates to the media, broadcasting, and entertainment industries.

- News content to be tested is broader in scope, covering selected local, regional, national, and global sources.

- The project will begin as soon as approval is received. Results will be reported six weeks after the end of the six-month pilot project.

Critical success factors

- Commitment from IRC, IT, Corporate Communications, and M&E to openly support the initiative and to send staff to attend project meetings, meet with information content vendor representatives, supply technology support, and test and evaluate the prototype.

- Funds to purchase services.

- IRC Manager being designated a member of the Portal Planning Team.

- Expectation management to explain that the IRC will no longer devote as much time to the *Taylor Twynne Today* service while staff time is diverted to the new prototype service.

Additional requirements

- Realign responsibilities of IRC staff.

- Assign staff person from IT as liaison for the prototype project.

- Hold meetings with vendor representatives, IT liaison, and M&E.

- Authorize (finance) an expenditure up to $25,000 and transfer the funds.

- Prepare news item about the project, for dissemination on the intranet, from the Director of Business Development to all practice group Directors and senior management (draft to be provided by IRC).

6. Budget and Cost Analysis

Direct Costs for Prototype Project

Content

The prototype project will incur costs for the subscription to global and industry news content and related tools. Variables include:

- Number of employees included in the subscriber license

- Content selected: cost of specific information content x number of content items selected

- Length of time content is stored locally and in what form

The pilot project will use a news and industry package with a range of monitoring capabilities but not requiring integration into our corporate intranet to get started (integration will occur later).

Based on discussions with other librarians and preliminary and informal discussion with the preferred content vendor, the content cost for the prototype is estimated to be $25,000–30,000 for six months.

Staffing

No new staffing is required for the prototype. Existing staff will be involved:

- One Information Professional will spend approximately 50 percent of her time on the project, primarily in working with M&E to identify resources for inclusion, in meeting with the content vendor to develop specific topical filter strategies, and in testing and evaluating the service.

- IRC Manager will spend approximately 20 percent of his time on overseeing the project, negotiating vendor terms and costs, and participating in Portal Planning Team meetings.

Project Costs and the Library Budget

There is no room in the current library budget to purchase additional news content as our existing service will be delivered for the duration of the project.

When next year's budget is being prepared, $35,000 will be diverted from the existing service to the new one.

Project Costs and Other Cost Centers

The Director of the M&E practice group has indicated he is willing to contribute $10,000 from current subscriptions in his department to the project.

The IT Department has budgeted funds for the portal development project. Integration of news content will leverage the expenditure on portal development and software. The cost of integration of news and business information content could logically be rolled into the budget allotted to portal development.

Costs for a Fully Implemented Company-wide *Issues and Industry Intelligence Service,* Subsequent to the Pilot

Content costs

Total costs for the full service are anticipated to be in the range of $95,000 based on two tiers of access:

1. Access to the news component by all employees: 300 seats x $150 annual license = $45,000 per year

2. In addition, access to selected company and industry components of the service by senior management, IRC, Consultants and their Administrative Assistants, and some others (with room for adding new seats within the first year): 250 seats x $200 annual license = $50,000 per year

New investment

Proposed Media Monitoring Service for all Taylor Twynne employees	$95,000
Less current monitoring services costs: - IRC purchase of content for *Taylor Twynne Today* - Corporate Services purchase of content for *TT in the News* and *TT Week in Review*	$30,000 $18,000
Total new investment:	$47,000

Technology

It is anticipated that when the service is delivered to all practice groups in the company, it will be integrated into the new company portal to allow a customized interface, more monitoring tools, and extensive capabilities for workflow integration. At that time, technical costs will be incurred in integrating the news into our portal software.

Staffing

It is anticipated that the IRC will need to hire one additional information professional to work closely with practice group personnel to identify and acquire resources, administer the media monitoring service, set up personalization and customization tools, and offer training and support—at an estimated salary of $70,000 plus benefits. That cost should be seen in light of the fact that the information professional will free up time for the Communications staff currently administering the existing news service.

7. Benefits

Productivity Gains

Appendix 4 is an abstract linking to a white paper prepared by a leading international research firm on knowledge workers' investment of time in information searching.

Extrapolation from that paper allows an approximation of the costs of seeking information at Taylor Twynne, as follows:

Average hours per knowledge worker per week searching for information	Cost per week, using average salary figures for and # of knowledge workers at TT	Cost per knowledge worker per year
9.5	$365	~$19,000

Employees at Taylor Twynne are experiencing lack of integrated access to information collections and lack of good content. They currently have to comb through hundreds of news stories collected in a minimum of two intranet locations when they need to retrieve a specific news item. To find company and industry information, they supplement their personal contacts with an even wider variety of secondary sources: bookmarked Web sites, print journals, personal "libraries," company documents, and the IRC's collection and reference service. Such laborious practices are extremely time-consuming.

Our proposed *Issues and Industry Intelligence Service* will ultimately have the capability to deliver, to his or her desktop, the tailored news and industry information every employee needs. The news content will be integrated with our internal enterprise content as well as other external information of value to the employee. The service will offer research as well as monitoring opportunities and thus not only help quality decision making but also protect against missing important information.

We estimate that if each knowledge worker at Taylor Twynne saves 2.5 hours per week in searching for information, the annual savings per knowledge worker will be almost $5,000. Using the number of Consultants and their Assistants (225), such savings roll up to a potential productivity gain of more than $1 million.

Competitive Advantage

We are planning a service with the capability to bring thousands of newswires, publications, transcripts, and company and industry reports from more than 100 countries to our employees' desktops. Taylor Twynne is known for hiring experts in its practice fields—we propose to give them the expert tools. The right information, at the right time, is a competitive advantage as the following occurrence illustrates:

> IRC staff has been attending the weekly meetings of the M&E practice group. At one such recent meeting, a potential client was discussed. Afterwards, the IRC Information Professional researched the client and in a source that offers pre-published content found a remarkable news item. Immediately upon getting this "heads up," we acted upon it, and reports are that it has led to promising discussions about an assignment.
>
> *Without the timely information we received from the IRC and its information resources, we wouldn't have had what we needed to approach this key potential client at the right time.*
> —Director, Media & Entertainment

Cost Per User Compared to Other Corporate Costs

As stated earlier, a trial news and industry package with a range of monitoring capabilities will cost an estimated $25,000–30,000 for six months for the M&E group. (IRC staff and Corporate Communications staff will also have access to the trial service.) The estimated per-user cost is thus $300 per user per month for the trial.

Such an investment compares favorably to costs for other corporate services. For example, average monthly communication costs (hotel Internet access, cell phones, PDAs) per employee were well in excess of this amount as reported for the last fiscal year.

As well, the cost per user for content typically decreases with higher numbers of users licensed to a product; hence the per-user cost will decline when all employees have access to the service.

Leveraging Technology Investments

The *Issues and Industry Intelligence Service* will maximize the planned investment in portal software. Now is the right time to proceed to maximize the ultimate benefit to knowledge workers.

8. Strategic Alignment

Alignment with Three Taylor Twynne Strategic Goals

Taylor Twynne's most recent annual report states the strategic priorities and refers to content management:

- Pursue growth in Asia Pacific (India and China), Central and Eastern Europe, and Latin America.
- Create opportunities for growth by adding to our industry sector specialization.
- Support growth by attracting and nurturing the most talented people in an environment where they enjoy great leadership and opportunities to develop exciting careers and competitive rewards within a contemporary workplace.

As our company grows, we need to reassess our IT strategies in order to invest in important infrastructure for control of our business processes, including content management.

The proposed pilot project is directly aligned with those strategic directions.

Project Impact on Other Taylor Twynne Groups and Initiatives

Communications group

- The Communications group will partner with IRC, IT, and M&E consultants to plan and deliver a prototype service.
- Communications group members are enthusiastic about the proposal because they have been experiencing problems with the service to which they currently subscribe. As well as giving input into the news content for the prototype, they will be key users of the new service.

IT department and portal planning team

- IT is a key stakeholder in the project.
- The prototype project will require limited IT support. The rollout of the full capability service across the company will need full IT collaboration and assistance.
- The new *Issues and Industry Intelligence Service* represents an opportunity for the portal development initiative to deliver leading edge information content and tools from day one.

Practice groups

- All practice groups are eager to have access to the service and resources M&E will receive.

- There may be some concern that the "newest" practice group is receiving the service first; it will be important to make the reasons for the pilot clear and to emphasize that the intention is to extend service across Taylor Twynne once the pilot learnings are in hand. (Note that we cannot permit an extension of access beyond the license purchased for the trial service.)
- It will be important to keep everyone in the company, and in particular all practice group Directors, informed about project developments and timelines.
- Our strategy will be to make a global news service available on all desktops as soon as possible after the trial, and then to work with individual practice groups to identify industry information requirements.

9. Readiness to Proceed

Steps Taken to Date

- Collaboration between the IRC and M&E group has created a foundation for the project.
- Informal discussions have taken place between the IRC Manager, the Chair of the Portal Planning Team, and the Corporate Communications Manager.
- The IRC Manager, who evaluated the services of several information providers in his previous workplace, has held informal discussions with the preferred vendor for the trial. The vendor's news product has been selected because it is built from multiple seamlessly integrated information services.
- IRC staff have planned realignment of job responsibilities to make time available for the project.

What Is Needed to Move Forward

- A staff person from IT being assigned as liaison for the prototype project.
- Authorization from Finance for an expenditure up to $25,000.
- Written communication about the project from the Director of Business Development to all practice group Directors and senior management.

Immediate Next Steps

- Realign responsibilities of IRC staff.
- Have IRC Manager, IT liaison, M&E, and Corporate Communications Manager meet Vendor representatives.

- Transfer funds from M&E to IRC budget.
- Prepare news item about project for dissemination on the intranet.

10. Appendices

Author's Note: The appendices Michael intends to include were described in the text of his proposal; the text of the appendices is therefore omitted.

Appendix 1: What industry journals are currently available at the desktop? What key journals are missing?
Appendix 2: Benchmark librarians who offered their insights on news monitoring
Appendix 3: List of relevant articles
Appendix 4: Abstract of white paper on knowledge workers' investment of time in information seeking

What's Next?

We cover tips on making effective presentations and feature Michael's PowerPoint slides.

CHAPTER 7

Presenting the Message in Person

Presentations are usually intended to provide the highlights from the content of a more comprehensive document. Thus, they tell a quick story, and interested parties may obtain further background and detail from the business case proper. Although it is possible some cultures support decision making by slides alone, it could be awkward to make a presentation without being able to point to a document with additional detail.

Here are some general tips for any business presentation.

On stage:

- **Put yourself in their shoes:** To present a case effectively, you must know who is in front of you. Do research so as to understand the perspective of your stakeholders. Think about the concerns and objectives on the part of decision makers, both those in the audience and those who may hear about the proposal secondhand.

- **Plan the key messages:** Avoid the trap of spending time on the operational detail spelled out in the proposal document. The amount of time you have to present—and to make your critical points—is limited. Highlight business benefits and outcomes rather than inputs and work steps.

- **Be aware of slide presentation fatigue on the part of the audience:** If you plan to use slides at all, limit the substantive ones to fewer than 10. Start with the strongest benefit, and show what results your ideas will bring.

- **Give decision makers a choice:** It sometimes eases the path to approval if there are alternatives. Although you emphasize the benefits of your proposed approach in your presentation, be prepared to speak about the "viable options" and their individual merits and costs.

- **Rehearse:** Practice rehearsing at least the first three minutes of your proposal presentation down to every sentence, managing the speed at which you speak. Ideally, you would rehearse the entire 15 minutes, but getting past the first three is key. In addition, be prepared for questions as you go along; you need to handle them appropriately (finding a balance between getting into detail too early and saying "that comes later") and get back on track.

Afterwards:

- **Don't stop communicating:** Selling your case is not over even when you have the "go-ahead" to proceed from management. You need to maintain buy-in also among those who will be tasked with implementing the project. To maintain momentum and support, communicate regular progress reports, quick wins, and milestones to all stakeholders.

Illustration: Michael's Slides

Using Case Study 3 in Chapter 6 as an example, we now take a look at the slides Michael prepared for his presentation to senior management.

The following slides do not reflect the corporate or independent graphics Michael—and you—would ordinarily employ. Good slide design is paramount, and fortunately, there are many resources to help achieve a professional, clean, yet attractive look.

Issues & Industry Intelligence Service

- Proposal to pilot a leading-edge global and industry news service for M&E
- To meet critical information needs supporting our growth and competitive edge—while cutting down wasted time
- Information and intelligence, tailored to TT knowledge workers, about …
  - our specialized industry sectors
  - competitors
  - customers
  - business partners
  - sourcing prospects

Drivers and Results

☐ From current situation …   ☐ To these results …

> Employees spending too much time seeking information
> Lack of global & industry news
> Duplication in costs & effort for media monitoring
> No access to news & information away from desktops

> 25% savings in the amount of time employees spend on seeking information
> Employees with "just in time, just the right" information
> Elimination of cost & effort: one entity responsible for media monitoring
> Information accessible outside the office on PDAs

Key Benefits

- Productivity gains
  - Cost of potential time savings = more than $1 million per year
- Competitive advantage
  - Attracting & keeping the "best staff in the business"
  - Competing for new clients/projects

Approach to the Project. IRC will ...

- Contract with a major content integrator for 6 months

- Work with M&E practice group to identify news & industry information

- Test personalized profiles for M&E personnel

- Continue, with Corp Comms, to supply media monitoring to all others

- Participate in Portal Planning Initiative toward integration of news content for all TT employees

Costs Are Low and Support Corporate Goals

- Modest cost per user
  - Lower than e.g., cell phone costs

- Leveraging technology investment
  - Objectives for new media monitoring service and portal initiative are identical

Budget

- Content costs for M&E personnel for 6 months ~ $25–30K

- Communications staff will have access

- $10K from M&E budget

- IRC budget continues to pay for existing media monitoring service

- Net new cost for future service for all employees ~ $47K/yr

Requirements & Next Steps

Requirements

- Finance authorization for $25K
- IT rep assigned to project
- IRC Manager a member of Portal Planning Team

Next Steps

- IRC manager to meet with vendor reps, IT liaison, M&E, and Communications staff
- Prepare news item about project for intranet

Questions, Comments?

- Michael Flint, extension 1234
- I will be happy to meet with you individually to provide more detail

CHAPTER 8

Appearance Matters

It could be argued that the appearance of your business plan should be immaterial—but in actuality, it is not! A visually undifferentiated or messy look demands too much work from the reader by interfering with comprehension; worse, it may act as a barrier to approval. Conversely, an easy-to-understand and appealing appearance aids in getting the message across.

The following examples are intended to illustrate how differently the same information can be presented. The reader may decide which is the preferable layout. If a corporate style is imposed on documents, there should still be opportunities to apply it in ways to maximize clarity.

The typical visual elements in professional documents include font and font size; special effects such as bolding and italics; lines or text boxes to set text apart; bullets and tables to array information for at-a-glance reading; and color (when it is expected the document will be printed in color).

The following is a snippet of text from a hypothetical business case, shown in several versions.

Version 1

Completely unformatted, the four paragraphs require the reader to read every sentence in order to gain an impression of what is being communicated.

Section 4. Access to internal information

Over the last five years, the number of projects has exploded, going from approximately 50 per year five years ago to 400 per year today. As a result, the associated documentation has become a challenge in terms of management and retrieval. Staff members say they spend a frustrating amount of time looking for documents pertaining to a given project and often stumble serendipitously on a more recent copy of a document they had found earlier. Not being able to be certain they have identified the "official" or "final" copy of a document or presentation introduces an uncomfortable level of uncertainty.

The current mechanisms for keeping documents and presentations include their being stored on personal hard drives, on departmental shared drives in subject folders, and in print form in the document room. Although the theory is that only "good" documents (the final, official versions that are to support historical activity review) are placed in the document room, anecdotal evidence says otherwise. For example, a new discovery can lead to a revision of a formerly "final" document, but the latest revision and the reasons for it may not be printed and filed due to the workload of the individual handling the file. While they are comfortable with personal filing systems on their own computers, staff members express difficulty in navigating the folder structure on the shared drives, often resorting to "brute force" word searches.

The rapid growth in document volumes has raised concerns that corporate memory is compromised so that opportunities for taking advantage of previous experience are lost. Staff members indicate they feel they are expending efforts needlessly to "reinvent the wheel" because they have no way to know that a particular type of project took place in the past—or no way to retrieve the documents pertaining to such a project if they did know it occurred.

Similarly, as the number of staff has risen dramatically as well, and as turnover has culled the ranks of individuals with long service, the effectiveness of informal personal information exchange has been lost. Unaware who is an expert in a given area, staff members perform a great deal of "asking around" before they find the right people to consult.

Version 2

Here, the boldface lead sentence for each paragraph signals its main theme. Readers are being oriented up front what the four areas of concern are.

Section 4. Access to internal information

Many more projects:
Over the last five years, the number of projects has exploded, going from approximately 50 per year five years ago to 400 per year today. As a result, the associated documentation has become a challenge in terms of management and retrieval. Staff members say they spend a frustrating amount of time looking for documents pertaining to a given project and often stumble serendipitously on a more recent copy of a document they had found earlier. Not being able to be certain they have identified the "official" or "final" copy of a document or presentation introduces an uncomfortable level of uncertainty.

Current document management is ineffective:
The current mechanisms for keeping documents and presentations include their being stored on personal hard drives, on departmental shared drives in subject folders, and in print form in the document room. Although the theory is that only "good" documents (the final, official versions that are to support historical activity review) are placed in the document room, anecdotal evidence says otherwise. For example, a new discovery can lead to a revision of a formerly "final" document, but the latest revision and the reasons for it may not be printed and filed due to the workload of the individual handling the file. While they are comfortable with personal filing systems on their own computers, staff members express difficulty in navigating the folder structure on the shared drives, often resorting to "brute force" word searches.

Corporate memory is compromised:
The rapid growth in document volumes has raised concerns that corporate memory is compromised so that opportunities for taking advantage of previous experience are lost. Staff members indicate they feel they are expending efforts needlessly to "reinvent the wheel" because they have no way to know that a particular type of project took place in the past—or no way to retrieve the documents pertaining to such a project if they did know it occurred.

Informal personal networks are less effective:
Similarly, as the number of staff has risen dramatically as well, and as turnover has culled the ranks of individuals with long service, the effectiveness of informal personal information exchange has been lost. Unaware who is an expert in a given area, staff members perform a great deal of "asking around" before they find the right people to consult.

Version 3

The spatial separation of the "main theme" from the accompanying narrative makes it easier for readers to see at a glance what the issues are because their eyes need only run down the left side of the table.

Section 4. Access to internal information	
Many more projects	Over the last five years, the number of projects has exploded, going from approximately 50 per year five years ago to 400 per year today. As a result, the associated documentation has become a challenge in terms of management and retrieval. Staff members say they spend a frustrating amount of time looking for documents pertaining to a given project and often stumble serendipitously on a more recent copy of a document they had found earlier. Not being able to be certain they have identified the "official" or "final" copy of a document or presentation introduces an uncomfortable level of uncertainty.
Current document management is ineffective	The current mechanisms for keeping documents and presentations include their being stored on personal hard drives, on departmental shared drives in subject folders, and in print form in the document room. Although the theory is that only "good" documents (the final, official versions that are to support historical activity review) are placed in the document room, anecdotal evidence says otherwise. For example, a new discovery can lead to a revision of a formerly "final" document, but the latest revision and the reasons for it may not be printed and filed due to the workload of the individual handling the file. While they are comfortable with personal filing systems on their own computers, staff members express difficulty in navigating the folder structure on the shared drives, often resorting to "brute force" word searches.
Corporate memory is compromised	The rapid growth in document volumes has raised concerns that corporate memory is compromised so that opportunities for taking advantage of previous experience are lost. Staff members indicate they feel they are expending efforts needlessly to "reinvent the wheel" because they have no way to know that a particular type of project took place in the past—or no way to retrieve the documents pertaining to such a project if they did know it occurred.
Informal personal networks are less effective	Similarly, as the number of staff has risen dramatically as well, and as turnover has culled the ranks of individuals with long service, the effectiveness of informal personal information exchange has been lost. Unaware who is an expert in a given area, staff members perform a great deal of "asking around" before they find the right people to consult.

Version 4

Setting out the main themes in bullet form further reduces the amount of time readers need to understand the message. Color could be used here to make a stronger visual impression that "this is section four."

Section 4. Access to internal information	
Many more projects	• Number of projects grown 50 to 400 per year in five years • Associated documentation is difficult to manage and find • Staff spend too much time looking for documents and can't be sure a document is the official one • Staff are not confident the correct document has been identified

Current document management is ineffective	• Documents and presentations stored …
	  - On personal hard drives
	  - On departmental shared drives in subject folders that are difficult to navigate—staff resort to "brute force" word searches
	• Document room intended to hold final copies, but subsequent revisions may not be filed due to workload

Corporate memory is compromised	• Lost opportunities for taking advantage of previous experience • Wheel reinvention • May not be able to find documents even if it is known a similar project took place earlier
Informal personal networks are less effective	• New headcount + turnover = loss of knowledge "who to go to" • Much "asking around" to identify the right people to consult

Afterword:
Final Checklist

Before you submit your case, you may want to take a step back and consider whether your document satisfies this checklist. If it does, it's ready to go!

- ☐ Did you review the materials in this guide to match each section of your document?

- ☐ If it's possible, have you had a colleague read the case and give input?

- ☐ Did you re-read your case—yet again?

  - Is your case not only factual but persuasive? Would you support this request if you were senior management?

  - Does the case seem too long? Could operational detail be omitted or placed in an appendix?

  - Are appropriate supporting data appended?

- ☐ Do you list specific data (usage indicators, current and estimated costs, time devoted to certain activities, etc.) rather than stating generalizations wherever possible?

- ☐ Have you anticipated questions or challenges likely to be raised, and have you incorporated answers to those questions in the body of your proposal? To get you thinking, here's a "devil's advocate" list of questions a *decision maker* could ask:

- I was not aware of any difficulty—**what**, exactly, will be better if I agree to this proposal?

- If as the decision maker I do nothing, what would be my **best and worst case** scenarios?

- Exactly **how** is your proposal going to improve the problem you describe?

- Isn't there a **cheaper** way to address the challenge at hand, if it's indeed a problem?

- Is there published or strong anecdotal **evidence** why going with your proposal is advisable?

- Am I a guinea pig? Have **similar organizations** achieved a payoff from a proposal like yours?

- How will we know we got our **money's worth**?

☐ Have you applied formatting to enhance readability and clarity?

About the Author

Starting in the late 1970s, Ulla de Stricker held information industry positions with responsibility in the areas of market education, client relations, and product design for electronic information services. Following that successful career, she established a consulting practice (www.destricker.com) in 1992 focusing on strategic planning for information and knowledge management. The practice assists clients in all sectors in dealing with the evolving challenges and opportunities resulting from developments in approaches to corporate memory, knowledge exchange, information access, and related organizational functions.

Ulla is a frequent and popular contributor to the information profession through conference presentations and workshops, articles, and association activities, and she is well known for her interest in promoting the value of information professionals.

Index

More Great Books from Information Today, Inc.

Intranets for Info Pros

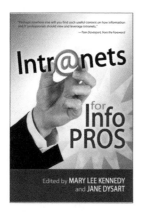

Edited by Mary Lee Kennedy and Jane Dysart

Foreword by Tom Davenport

The intranet is among the primary landscapes in which information-based work occurs, yet many info pros continue to view it with equal parts skepticism and dread. In *Intranets for Info Pros*, editors Mary Lee Kennedy and Jane Dysart and 10 expert contributors provide support and encouragement to the information professional responsible for implementing or contributing to an intranet. Chapters demonstrate the intranet's strategic value, describe important trends and best practices, and equip info pros to make a key contribution to their organization's intranet success.

304 pp/softbound/ISBN 978-1-57387-309-3 $39.50

The Accidental Fundraiser

By Julie M. Still

Many nonprofit, charitable, and other small organizations need funding yet cannot afford to employ a full-time fundraiser, relying instead on volunteers or staff members to raise the money. *The Accidental Fundraiser* is a practical guide covering all aspects of fundraising for the small organization, the volunteer, and the staff person in any setting who plans to take on a fundraising project for which he or she may not have been trained. Julie Still offers practical and reassuring advice that will help any individual become an effective fundraiser regardless of previous experience.

176 pp/softbound/ISBN 978-1-57387-263-8 $29.50

The Thriving Library
Successful Strategies for Challenging Times

By Marylaine Block

Here is a highly readable guide to strategies and projects that have helped more than 100 public libraries gain community support and funding during challenging times. The author integrates survey responses from innovative library directors with her research, analysis, and extended interviews to showcase hundreds of winning programs and services. The strategies explored include youth services, partnerships, marketing, Library 2.0, and outreach.

352 pp/softbound/ISBN 978-1-57387-277-5 $39.50

Information Tomorrow
Reflections on Technology and the Future of Public and Academic Libraries

Edited by Rachel Singer Gordon

In *Informtion Tomorrow*, Rachel Singer Gordon brings together 20 of today's top thinkers on the intersections between libraries and technology. They address ways in which new technologies are impacting library services and share their ideas for using technology to meet patrons where they are. *Information Tomorrow* offers an engaging discussion for systems librarians, library IT workers, and library managers and administrators.

280 pp/softbound/ISBN 978-1-57387-303-1 $35.00